for
Billy Riley
"meus amicus semper"/
from

JC

2 May '94

see p 74

Columns Left
A Legacy to
Chattanooga

Bell Buckle, Tennessee

**By
Jac
Chambliss**

Library of Congress Cataloging-in-Publication Data

Chambliss, Jac, 1910-
    Columns left: a Chattanooga legacy/by Jac Chambliss
        p. cm.
    A collection of columns, many of which originally appeared in
Chattanooga news, Chattanooga times, and Chattanooga news free
press.
    ISBN 0-916078-34-5
    1. Chattanooga (Tenn.) I. Title.
F444.C445C43   1994
976.8'82—dc20

                                        93-42556
                                        CIP

Cover by Holly Lentz-Hays, Murfreesboro, Tennessee.

Dedication

This book is dedicated to the memory of my friend Alfred D. Mynders, whose encouragement and acceptance of my writings led me to continuing efforts to articulate what I feel and believe.

Preface

For more than a half-century I have been sending columns to the local press—the *Chattanooga News,* the *Chattanooga Times,* and the *Chattanooga News-Free Press.*

From time to time, friends have suggested that I collect and publish some of these columns, and I finally decided to put together in approximately chronological order those herein. The first was written in 1937.

I am grateful to the editors of the Chattanooga News, Times, and News-Free Press for publishing most of these writings. (Some have never before been published.)

I am also grateful to my wife Bena, who for over half a century has clipped and collected the columns; to my friend George W. Brown, who has been of great assistance in selecting and arranging them for publication; and to my secretary, Lorraine Geer, who typed and helped me compose many of them.

1930 - 1940

To a Small Tailor

Above the door of the tailor shop, the small red and black sign swayed in the October wind. Never the sky more blue, the sun more gold. On the door under the sign there hung a spray of flowers, in their midst a card that read: "Closed on account of the death of John Ott."

A few bright leaves tumbled through the cool, stirring air and scraped along the dark asphalt of the street. The captains and the kings depart—and now John Ott.

He was a little tailor, born in Alsace-Lorraine almost seventy years ago. His father was a stone-cutter, and during the months of the late Spring would often leave the house after supper and be gone all night, wandering through the forest to hear the song of the nightingale and to eat the crimson fruit of the wild strawberries that grew there. Sometimes John Ott spoke of his leaving his home when he was but a lad, and of gazing back at the disappearing town as the train pounded around the curve of the river, and of how his eyes ached with the hot tears.

With his dexterous fingers he fashioned many a garment for those who still refuted the mechanization of tailoring, and who perhaps foolishly preferred the feel of cloth that was hand sewn. With keen wit he fashioned many a phrase that delighted those who still believed in the outworn creed of individualism, not yet having learned that the world owed them their livelihood. Especially we recall the flavor of certain of his recent remarks concerning Hitler who, incidentally, was born only a few miles from the little tailor's birthplace.

We had intended going to see him after noticing a few days ago the neatly lettered card in his shop window: "Temporarily closed on account of illness." Death stole a march on us, as so often he does.

Lest this be thought much ado about nothing, we recommend to your attention the list of John Ott's pallbearers. We join with them and with a host of others in paying tribute to a small tailor who had become a symbol of the nobility of the artisan—a small tailor upon whose shop door hangs a spray of flowers that spread their vanishing fragrance on the blue winds of October.

At the Symphony

There were ten bass viols standing in a row. There was a golden harp a little to the left of center. In the right rear were the drums and cymbals. In the center front was a man with a silver flute and another man with a slender, black oboe. And all around, spread in semicircular rows, were the violins, the players sitting in ordered ranks.

The lights went down. A hush fell. The hands of the violinists rose in unison. Then out of the silence was spun music. Like a stream it flowed, now glittering in the sun, now flecked as by the shadow of leaves, now whipped into waves by the lash of a black-maned wind.

Through Beethoven's "Overture to Leonore," his "Symphony No. 5 in C Minor," through Harris' "Three Pieces for Orchestra," and Delius' "The Walk to the Paradise Garden," it flowed, and then into the faery loveliness of Strauss' "Tales From the Vienna Woods." The symmetry of the waltz time seemed to arrange the color of the music more surely. Once, near the end, when the forest of the violins was stilled, there was only a tiny stream of water-pure, limpid sound that the flute caught and held.

And so the program was completed. But the applause of the thousands in the audience roared on and on. At times it seemed almost that the very chairs were shaking with the thunder of it. It pounded against the walls and ceiling to fall crashing. Then, as an encore came the scherzo from Mendelssohn's "Midsummer Night's Dream."

And last of all, in final encore came Sousa's immortal "Stars and Stripes Forever."

Now there was a queer thing about that. This was common music—music that was familiar, that touched the nostalgic area of one's sentimental cosmos.

It seemed that he was a boy on a green parade ground at Lexington, Virginia. The golden fingers of a long-vanished afternoon sun warmed the cadet gray of his coatee, its reflection glinting off the polished brass knobs of his cartridge box and various buckles. The quiet air still trembled with the reverberations of the evening gun. Far down to the right, a little band of straggling musicians was preparing to start the music to which the corps would pass in review. There were two thumps on the bass drum and then—the "Starts and Stripes Forever"!

He could feel his whiskers growing as wave after wave of emotion swept over him. There was a dim, wind-blown cry: "Battalion!" Then "Company!" bawled the captains. "Platoon!" barked the lieutenants. There was a pause. "Squads right!" came the dim cry, echoing down the lines. Rifles were gripped more tightly between thumbs and fingers. "March!"

Right shoulder arms and simultaneously right face, marking time for four beats. Then step off. So to the end of the parade ground, and then a column left and a squads left into line, and on down the field. The music soared and trilled and thumped and whistled. The boy glanced from under the visor of his shako, now right, now left. It was a pretty fair line. They were almost in front of the reviewing stand.

"Eyes . . . right!" yelled B company captain, and every head jerked to the right. The boy stuck his tongue inside his lower lip to tighten the grip on his chin strap. The line swung past in review, the white-gloved hands swinging in unison, the rifle butts held even, the cadet gray trousers, black-striped, forming a perfect line.

"Front!" Each head snapped back, face forward. They had passed in review. The job was done. Their shadows marched ahead of them, blue upon the sun-gilt green of the grass. The statue of Stonewall Jackson loomed before them and back of it the time-worn walls of the Institute, with a glory of clouds above.

And then it was gone.

The little man with the graceful arms and the baton in his hand was bowing from his pedestal. People were struggling into overcoats. The Symphony was over.

October Prayers

The earth turns. The sun slides to the south. And in October's heart there is faint-echoed perfume of autumn's harvest, of the sweet-scented rains of June and the blowing blossoms of April. The wood is aflame. The maples pour their scarlet on the cool blue air. The hickories are lemon yellow, the dogwood a deep russet. Some of the leaves are brown and dead.

My brother is an Aviation Intelligence officer. The other day, one fair October afternoon, he went for a flight in a B-26 bomber with a pilot friend. The bomber is a huge, squat, powerful and exceedingly heavy machine, with blunt wings, and requires a high take-off and landing speed.

My brother sat immediately behind the pilot and co-pilot as they taxied the great plane to the very end of the runway and headed into the wind. The motors revved up. The ship quivered and roared. Then the brakes released and it began to pour down the runway in an ever increasing torrent of speed. My brother watched the pilot, whose hands were flickering over the myriad controls. The pilot's face was tense, drawn. Perspiration beaded on his forehead and trickled down his cheeks and he cursed in a cold, impersonal monotone. He cursed blasphemously, but not in anger.

Then the stubby-winged monster nosed into the air and the tension was gone. Below the plane the bright October color of the earth flowed past. And my brother knew then that the pilot's cursing was in a sense a prayer, and that it had been answered.

But a few days ago something else happened. In Detroit there is a place where two parallel tracks cross a street. Every morning at a certain time a passenger train crosses this street at a high speed. As the thundering locomotive nears the street, the engineer, seated high up in the cab, watches the crossing with keen, anxious eyes, while the hoarse blast of the whistle screams warning to those near at hand and cries a prayer into the distant heavens.

On this particular morning the train's way led through the fantastic fairyland of October's color. The death-stained leaves made gay the woods and hills, the fields and hollows past which the steam engine fled.

The engineer looked quiet-eyed at the color of the wood, the bright and shining loveliness of the October day. At his back lay the coaches, the Pullmans full of people whose destiny and safekeeping rested in his gloved hand that now lay quiet on the throttle. Ahead of him stretched the ribbons of rail. As his locomotive approached this particular crossing, it met and passed a freight train on the other track thundering by in the opposite direction.

The engineer's face was tight, tense. The locomotive screamed and screamed again, that same tocsin, that same windy blown prayer that had been answered so many times. But on this day and at this hour— perhaps God was asleep. At any rate, a bus lumbered across immediately in the path of the engine. A bus full of children. Nineteen were killed. The train slid to a halt.

And so the earth turns. The wood is aflame. Who knows what prayers drift heavenward through this blue and smoky air? Who knows which will be answered, which will not? For some of the leaves are brown and dead, and even the bright ones make sad music in some hearts.

Stephen Vincent Benet

It has become cliché to say that "John Brown's Body" constitutes the nearest approach to an epic that has been produced in the United States. And yet through the worn texture of the very words, the truth shines and cannot be denied. Only the small mind denies the truth often found in the trite language of common possession.

It is to be regretted that Benet—like Thomas Wolfe—should have died at such and early age. One cannot but speculate as to what heights would have been attained had death not intervened. How often the steep white cliffs of morning echo the tolling bell!

To some, poetry is an artifice. To Benet, it was an emotion. In his writings one finds a grateful lack of the stylized artificiality that characterizes so much of our so-called poetry. There is a musical flow, a natural balance that is fundamentally sound and pleasing. And he also possessed a rare and invaluable ability of understatement. Too many are inclined to go gnat-hunting with shotguns.

Those familiar with "John Brown's Body" will recall the vivid coloring of the pages where Pickett's charge at Gettysburg is described:

"I shall go forward, sir" he said and turned to his men:
The commands went down the line. The gray ranks started to move.
  Slowly at first, then faster, in order, stepping like deer,
The Virginians, the fifteen thousand, the seventh wave of the tide.
  There was a death-torn mile of broken ground to cross,
And a low stone wall at the end, and behind it the Second Corps
And behind that force another, fresh men who had not yet fought.
They started to cross that ground. The guns began to tear them.

From the hill they say that it seemed more like a sea than a wave,
  A sea continually torn by stones flung out of the sky,
  And yet, as it came, still closing, closing and rolling on,
  As the moving sea closes over the flaws and rips of the tide.
You could mark the path that they took by the dead that they left behind,
Spilled from that deadly march as a cart spills meal on a road.

And yet they came on unceasing, the fifteen thousand no more,
And the blue Virginia flag did not fall, did not fall, did not fall.

I know of no other place in literature where the desperate poignance
of battle has been more aptly snared in simple words.

The other day I had occasion to pick up a thin black-bound book of
Benet's verse published in 1936 under the title *Burning City*. In it are
two poems that are particularly interesting. The first is entitled "Thanks,"
and constitutes a sort of grace, or thanksgiving. In its spontaneity and
naturalness, it expresses more eloquently than could anything else the
true poetic genius of its author:

For these my thanks, not that I eat or sleep,
Sweat or survive, but that at seventeen
I could so blind myself in writing verse
That the wall shuddered and the cry came forth
And the numb hand that wrote was not my hand
But a wise animal's.
Then the exhaustion and the utter sleep.
O flagrant and unnecessary body,
So hard beset, so clumsy in your skill!
For these my thanks, not that I breathe and ache,
Talk with my kind, swim in the naked sea,
But that the tired monster keeps the road
And even now, even at thirty-eight,
The metal heats, the flesh grows numb again
And I can still go muttering down the street
Not seeing the interminable world
Nor the ape faces, only the live coal.

The other poem is one of the most moving presentations of every day
drama I ever read. And today, with Stephen gone, it must have special
sanctity to Rosemary, Stephen's young and talented widow:

The Lost Wife

In the daytime, maybe your heart's not breaking,
For there's the sun and sky and working
And the neighbors to give you a word or hear you,
but, ah, the long nights when the wind comes shaking
The cold, black curtain, pulling and jerking,
And no one there in the bed to be near you.

And worse than the clods on the coffin falling
Are the clothes in the closet that no one wears now
And the things like hairpins you're always finding.
And you wouldn't mind the ghost of her calling
As much as knowing that no one cares now
If the carpet fades when the sun gets blinding.

I look in the houses, when twilight narrows,
And in each a man comes back to a woman.
The thought of that coming has spurs to ride me.
—Death, you have taken the great like sparrows,
But she was so slight, so small, so human.
You might have left her to lie beside me.

Late Autumn

In the dying wood the chords of color sound their symphony, scarlet and orange, lemon and russet, green and brown. Man walks across the dry, age-bitten earth, scraping beneath his leathern soles the fallen leaves, his eyes bright with their anguished color, his ears full of their death rattle, his nostrils assailed by their spiced and fading fragrance. And because he is man and hence bears inherent a small spark of Godhood, he is not filled with sadness at this mortal time, but merely with sweet nostalgia and with a fierce mounting exultancy for the conflict that is to come—that bitter conflict with the sharp-toothed frost and the desolate winter.

Now is the time of giant winds that shake the trees, the death-stained trees, by night. The howling of those winds fills all the midnight void, and the dark air is full of the tossing of tortured boughs. Lying abed, one hears the wooden-thudding hail of acorns. And now at night there is the red-eyed fire that flares and dies upon the hearth, speaking in small flattering syllables of blue and yellow flame and bringing to life upon dim ceilings and walls shadows that change and swarm with magic mildness. And now, also, at night there falls through the cold and turbulent darkness the feathered crying of the south-bent birds. Something there is of kinship in the heart of the insistent hunger of these pilgrims!

But most of all, this is the time of perfect dawn and dusk. Aldous Huxley has truly said:

"The horizontal light of evening causes the world to shine with such an unusual, such a goldenly improbable radiance, that, looking, we are startled out of our ordinary purblind complacency; we are almost forced to see things as they really are and not as we imagined them to be. Or rather, since we cannot see things as they really are, we are forced to become aware of our immediate impressions and to forget the phantom generalizations and symbols which constitute our everyday universe."

The same is no less true of dawn.

Now is not yet the time of winter when from the lonely heart one well may cry:

Sharp-etched upon the cobalt air
        The sunlight-lacquered branches
             fly;
My heart is frozen with despair,
        And cold and senseless as the
           sky.

No. If ever the heart be sensate, it is now. Sensate of all the fleeting loveliness of earth. Sensate of time's swift flight and of the imminence of death and the long sleeping. Yet sensate above all else of the great wheel of the year that turns and turns and will not stop—of the wheel that says:

"Nor winter's thorny chill, nor war, nor death of love, nor very death itself, can check the coming of the April dawn!"

WORLD WAR II

Metamorphosis

"Day alters; seasons alter; we
walking the wet rut, alter too."
—A. MacLeish

One of the qualities that endeared Thomas Wolfe to so many of us was his extreme sensitivity to the element of time in our lives. Those less hardy fear time and the change that inevitably accompanies the turning of the great wheel. To others—perhaps more brave—perhaps merely more foolhardy—it means the romance of metamorphosis; the experience of alteration.

At the moment we are in the process of being drastically and visibly altered. From an unwieldy mass of forlorn, bewildered and obtuse recruits we are being transformed into a company of disciplined, well-drilled apprentice seamen. Outwardly we are uniform in navy blues, khaki leggins ("boots") and regulation haircuts. (The haircuts, by the way, take one and a half minutes and most of the hair.)

There are many impressions and experiences that are sharp and clear and well worth recording. The ultra-efficiency of a staff that can pour recruits through their induction in such staggering numbers; the miracle of feeding thousands of men in a relatively small mess hall in a short space of time; the natural emergence of men of leadership and their assumption of responsibility—even the responsibility of roughly comforting the kid of 16 who has never been away from his mother before; all these are indelibly printed upon the recording mechanism of the mind and memory.

And in the realm of sensory impressions, there are just as many; the beauty of blue-clad and booted figures swinging by through the glittery white morning in step to the hard clear clatter of a drum, the walk to the canteen by night through the deep snow, the shoes creaking on the hard-packed path; the feathery snowflakes touching the face with cold kisses out of the cloud-packed night.

And attending church in a huge auditorium with a thousand bluejackets singing "The Battle Hymn of the Republic"—"as He died to make men holy, let us die to set men free." (And I hope that those who don't die will live to set men free!)

Then—sudden and sharp like a knife in the heart, the remembrance of things past; the feel of a horse; the gesture of a friend; a sudden glimpse of hair blown by the wind, the smooth cold fire of hands upon the face; and, printed upon the flowering dark, the thin pale sickle of a moon caught in a tangled web of twiggy trees.

So it goes. The moving finger writes—and the lines of men move on, their hearts ballooned with hope and fear, joy and sorrow, life and death.

To have heard, to have felt, to have seen all this and the imminence of all that lies ahead, spells out the logic of the time to come—that time when there will be indeed, peace on earth for men of good will!

Ovid began his Metamorphosis with the assertion that the first age was the golden age. In this real life Metamorphosis we may at least hope that at the end, we may attain an age more nearly golden than the past.

—But Never Quite Forgotten

It is a fortunate accident when a John Donne emerges from the sea of time to provide a careful blend of the heart that is delicately sensate to both flesh and spirit. There has recently been a renaissance in the popularity of that lusty English cleric who penned the immortal "And therefore never send to know for whom the bell tolls; it tolls for thee!"—and the unabashed love poems for which he is even more famous. It is a gracious occasion when one meets with such a figure, either in the realm of letters or in the flesh. There is a renewal of an old theme that seems to linger on in overtone from our childhood; a faith that flowered "when all the world was young, lad, and all the grass was green!"

Some of us who cling to the vestige of that antique faith doubt our ability to correctly proportion our energies and our receptivities. It is so easy to simply relax—to lift and drop with the waves. There is grave danger that the love of sensory impression may overbalance the more difficult and tortuous effort of metaphysical development—although it is easily apparent that such would be an error.

Today is July 4, 1944. We spent it just as any other day—there was no holiday. At 6:25 we marched to breakfast in a gray-uniformed line by devious paths that lay pale under a pale blue morning sky, past massive tree and well-trimmed hedge, past ivied wall and rolling lawn where the fresh-minted gold of the early sun slanted mistily down to shed its precious lacquering light upon the dewy grass.

All day we were in class or drilling or playing baseball on the lower playing field. A mellow peacefulness overhung the countryside, broken only by the musical tolling of the bells that are the calls to classes.

Then in the late afternoon we repaired to the stagroom of the Tavern—that low-ceiled subterranean place of cool, wood-paneled gloom, of yellow lights, small and discreet, of great wooden tables, carved and battered, of heavy wooden chairs, strong and generously comfortable. The air was full of the rich aroma of beer that foamed cold and clear and heady in the tankards, and the hum of mantalk and the silver tinkling behind the long bar. The white-vested waiters moved soundlessly about. The broiled bass was excellent. The total effect was altogether pleasing.

As we left, the remembrance of the date came back. The Fourth of July. It seemed so irrelevant—so beside the point.

Somehow the very phrase "the Fourth of July" mocked of heat and noise and picnickers and overcrowded automobiles and other dismal facts and circumstances.

We passed through the tall gateway, with webbed wrought-iron gates on either side, then walked slowly by Nassau Hall and came to the Union.

As we went in, someone was playing a piano in the little octagonal room that is hitched onto the Union. It was a boy of about 17. He was playing Clair de Lune, and the broken, crystal music spilled onto the blue warm air of early evening as cool, as refreshing as water from a cold mountain spring.

He was a muscular boy, and when he stopped playing we learned, to our pleasure, that he was quite a wrestler. Something about that fact touched a chord, seemed to wake a half-remembered dream; the Greek ideal—"the golden isles"—the accident of fate that could produce a Donne.

We left, went to our room and reread an article in the *New Yorker* about Judge Learned Hand of the United States Circuit Court of Appeals, and a speech he made last May on the occasion of an "I Am An American" Day celebration at Central Park in New York City.

You may have read the speech in last week's *Life*. If you haven't, you should. It is a great document. It has the simplicity, the earthy plainness and honesty of Lincoln in his little talk at Gettysburg. It has the poetry of Steve Benet. It has the religious awe and humility and devotion of a man who is great and who is better-than-average acquainted with God.

Among other things, he said this: "Liberty lies in the hearts of men and women; when it dies there, no Constitution, no law, no court can even do much to help it. . . . The spirit of liberty is the spirit which is not too sure that it is right; the spirit of liberty is the spirit which seeks to understand the minds of other men and women; the spirit of liberty is the spirit which weighs their interests alongside its own without bias; the spirit of liberty remembers that not even a sparrow falls to earth unheeded; the spirit of liberty is the spirit of Him, who, near two thousand years ago, taught mankind that lesson it has never learned but has never quite forgotten: that there may be a kingdom where the least shall be heard and considered side by side with the greatest."

Then I knew why it was that we go on having a Fourth of July in spite of the heat and the poison ivy and the ants in the sandwiches and the sand in the hair. It stands for something—for that something that is liberty, which mankind has never learned, but never quite forgotten.

The Essence Of Nostalgia

Never before has there been so much homesickness abroad in the earth. But, did you ever stop to think what the essence of homesickness—of nostalgia—really is?

The millions who are in uniform furnish perhaps the best opportunity for observation of the subjective and objective characteristics of that certain sickness of the heart!

You may have seen the lean, bronzed lieutenants from the convoys that ply the Seven Seas from the ice-haunted wastes of the Murmansk run to the heat-glazed doldrums of the Marianas. You may have seen the combat pilots who have come back with their young faces lined, their hair prematurely gray. I have seen them—watched them pace the concrete seawall where the warm, winking Gulf shoulders its way in from the blue Caribbean.

I have talked with them while the sunset burned out in the west and night came up out of the sea and swallowed the flat, sandy, low country.

And they are even as you and I would be—hurt, lost and afraid.

Here is the way they think: you go into Biloxi and it's a honky-tonk town, and there's a carnival and the penny-pitch games and the hard-faced women and the weak-faced men. There is the galaxy of red and green neon lights and the juke boxes and the hot, sweaty places where you go to buy beer and drinks, and you feel your mind retreating into itself, and your pure ego goes far away and is like a balloon, tethered to your body by a line, and it's very far away and you forget about the place where you are.

Then, maybe, you see a profile, and it has the clear, chiseled look of someone you loved and lost, and your mind flashes back across the days and months and years and you sit staring into space and remembering. You remember all sorts of things, but, chiefly, the impressions of the senses.

Things like these:

The smell of the grape arbor in midsummer, the purple grapes, dusty and ripe, the red grapes cool, firm, sweet to the tongue.

The sound of the churn being turned downstairs in the kitchen, and the slam of the screen door that opens onto the backyard.

The early morning, the cool of the air, the clean blue of the sky past the familiar leaves of the familiar tree outside the familiar window, and the whistle of the cardinal, and the strange, fugitive cry of the bluejay—that cry that sounds like "Monteagle! Monteagle! Monteagle!"

The tennis court in the late afternoon, with the shadows falling long and blue across the cooling red clay with its white lines, and the white tennis balls and the clean, chocking sound when the racquet hits them.

The bemused and lilac-shadowed dusk, when sounds the strictly silver and ever-so-light fluting of the hermit thrush, lost in the darkening wood.

The eery throttled cry of the weatherstripping under the front door when the rain and the wind blew from the east—and the desperate sobbing of the wind.

The old and almost lost remembrance of the crunching sound of the iron-tired wagon on the gravel of the road; the sturdy thudding of the horses' hooves; the long melodious call of the iceman; the creaking of a gate; the hum of the bees high up in the blossoming persimmon trees in June.

Your father's shoes beside your own small ones when you were in church, leaning forward, supposed to be listening to the long-drawn prayer; and the rough feel of your father's face when he put you to bed and kissed you goodnight.

The smell of the air before the rain; the clean, cold, intoxicating ozone smell with the imminence of storm, and running to the barn, the rich, sharp smell of leather and axle grease and horses; the dusty fragrance of the hay in the loft; the sound of the startled rain spattering sudden and heavy on the roof overhead.

These are things that are the essence of nostalgia: the little, forgotten impressions of sound and sight and taste and smell. And when men leave the crimson chorus of the guns and come again, these are the objectives they will seek.

You have read of this and that young hero who has come home and wandered about like a lost soul, dissatisfied and unhappy. It is because of this nostalgia—this homesickness—that neither time nor place can mend. They are changed, these boys, these men, and do not know it. They fail to realize that because they are changed, they cannot fit back into place as smoothly as a worn glove or a comfortable shoe. And so they seek again the door they cannot find, the word that is locked in the dim-lettered pages of the past—not knowing that the object of their quest, the essence of this nostalgia, exists only in their hearts. Which is really the safest place, after all.

New Orleans

A night in that strange city called New Orleans—that neon-lighted welter of ugliness and beauty, that strumpet city of the painted face whose body is diseased with poverty and filth:

We had walked along the river where it shoulders past the end of broad Canal Street, and had turned left and down river to the Vieux Carré. Past shadowy, dark-looming warehouses, strong with the golden-brown fragrance of coffee, the fermented, pig-sty smell of unrefined sugar, past lonely night-fogged buildings we went until we saw the glitter of the lights and came to the long shed-like market. There were the names: Batistella, Scontrino, Fertita; the fish-markets full of the salty, clamorous stink of the fish; the fruit and vegetable stands, with their mellow sunny smell; the chicken mart, with its warm feathery, sour odor—and so on and across the cobbled street to the Morning Call Coffee Shop, the place of marble counters, the clink of dishes, the hum of voices—and reigning over all, the blank-faced Register Clock, old as time itself, leering down from the wall on all the warmth and gaiety that held so firm against the chilled dark of the December night outside, where already a few large raindrops were spattering ominously down. And so we left, stepping into the night again, and as we did, a fugitive wind fled like a frightened ghost down the dark street, and we knew the rain was close. Past Jackson Square we walked, and then, at St. Louis Cathedral, turned right up Pirate's Alley. The broad sloping flagstones were dim in the darkness. A handful of dead leaves made dry scraping sounds as the wind herded them into the deeper shadows. As we turned into Royal Street, we met the rain, and upturning our collars, we hurried on along the uneven sidewalks, past drunken lampposts burning in the slant lines of the rain, past latticed windows, the webbed lacery of iron grillwork, rusty and worn, until at last we reached a door set in a thick wall, and we knocked, and the door swung open, and we entered.

We were greeted gravely, decorously, and ceremoniously by a mannered, discrete and liveried headwaiter, who, having relieved us of our rain-dripping topcoats, led the way to a table. It was small, white-linened. And in that ancient place, low-ceiled, thick-walled and mellow, the only lights were the petalled flames of red candles that bloomed golden in the gentle air. The walls were smoked with the slow burning of centuries, and the wine was pale gold as April sunlight, and it touched our hearts with faint sweet sadness for Aprils long since spent. We sat for a long time disposing the tender luscious cookery set before us—the gumbo, rich with tomato, shrimp, oyster, okra, and herb-flavored, with a rich roux and soft, well-cooked rice to thicken it. The trout, broiled to a rich gold, butter-sweet, with a tiny pyramid of cut lemon to give it a tang; the artichokes, tender, steamily done, with a fine lemon-and-butter sauce to dip the leaves in, one by one, and at the last, to soak the cream rich heart; the combination salad, with chopped cress and lettuce and egg, with bits of shrimp mixed in, and the whole deliciously flavored by a tart dressing; and finally, the ices and the demitasse.

And all the while we were there the heavy winter rain fell in the city outside, and we heard it crying in the darkness, beating against the windowpanes and the thick, sturdy walls.

And we were in love, and the flavor of that time was bitter-sweet like rose leaves; and we were moon-struck and slightly, sensuously daft like the names of the streets of that city: Bourbon, Chartres, Desire, and Cemeteries.

Mountain Man

The old man gripped the wheel loosely, glancing now and then at the compass where the illuminated numbers moved gravely from port to starboard and back again across the lubber's line. The ship moved with ponderous rolling dignity across the little hills of the mid-Pacific. The gray air blew cool and dank in their faces.

"Yes, sir," he said, and his voice sounded like a rusty cornet blown lightly—"I'm from Elkmont."

"Is that the place where all the conventions are—the church meetings?" asked the lieutenant, eyeing the weather-beaten face of the helmsman curiously.

"No, sir, you're thinking about Montreat," said the old man. He was chewing gum and his jaws moved regularly, opening and closing the wrinkles in his cheeks like the bellows of an accordion.

"How far is Gatlinburg from Elkmont?" asked the Lieutenant.

"It's nigh onto seven mile," replied the old man.

"Oh, I know where that is," said the lieutenant. "I remember going there when three of us drove up to Clingman's Dome and left the car and packmarched across the trail to Siler's Bald. That was back in '39."

The seconds of silence that followed swept in the remembrance of it all: the difficult hike, staggering along under the heavy packs; the immensities of space that lay to either hand as the trail wound brokenly along the razor-backed ridge; the copper-red light of the dying sun that shone with such luminous splendor through the red-rooted evergreens where dark shadows were already melting into the deepening dusk; the sharp green fragrance of spruce and pine; the fresh bear dung in the rocky path, and the slight tightening of the chords of the heart when it was seen; the anguished climb up the bald itself in the uncertainty of first dark, sweat dripping off the face, the back throbbing with the pain of it—and at the top, the sprawling out in the deep, soft grass under the sky; the dark blue of the sky, and the stars that burned in its depths, and the one planet that glowed red on the horizon. It was Mars, said William.

It was the day Germany invaded Poland. And now William was a major on the western front, and Pat had gone in the army, and here I

28

am, thought the lieutenant, in the middle of the Pacific Ocean. He shook himself.

The old man was speaking again. "A many a time I've walked the ridge along there," he said. "They was a time me an' my boy went up the mountain by Jake's Creek, across Big Smokey that lies 'twixt Clingman's and the Bald, along the ridge to Indian Gap and down to the Indian reservation."

"I have a friend," said the lieutenant, "who was raised in that country."

The old man spun the wheel.

"What's his name." he asked.

"His name's Dunn. He's with the Park Service."

"Yeah. I know him. Name's Charlie, ain't it?"

"I believe it is," said the lieutenant. "He lives in Chattanooga now. Stationed there."

His mind sought, captured instantly the gently rolling lawn-dressed hill where the Park building stood, out past Oglethorpe; the white columns of the building; the wooded stretches of Chickamauga Park with its hills and meadows, and the gray stone tower that lifted high into the fragile air—that tower whose winding stony stair one might ascend and view the grassy mead spread like a still, green sea away to the east. The wind might blow darkly and small rain come, but —

"I knowed most all the people that lived 'round there," the old man continued. "They was a time when people was a tougher breed than now. I had a summer hotel oncet. I lost it because in them days they wont no automobiles an' you could only keep it open fer a short time in the summers, an' they was too much money invested in it, but in the winter I had to keep someone in it. I had a family, they was a old woman no biggern that"—he indicated with his hand—"an' she had boys that ud mighty near make two o' you, an' she used to make all the clothes, even the shoes. She'd tan the hides an' cut out the pegs, an' she an' the little uns ud do the farmin' an' keep the house. An' she even shaved the old man. Every oncet in a while they'd gather a bit o' corn or some chestnuts an' put 'em in a waggin an' drive into Knoxville an' peddle 'em. Then they'd buy salt an' a mite o' this an' that. That's all they needed."

The lieutenant pondered, seeing again the massive stillness, the couchant power of those panther-graceful mountains, hearing again the deep, brooding silence of the ridgetops, remembering a tiny red spider that climbed up through the forest of the tall, green grass that grew on Siler's meadow, and the day that the three of them had lain there in the golden flood of the September sun, reciting limericks and imagining that they were a half inch tall and lost in the jungles of the grass.

"Did you ever hear of a man that lived there many years ago that wrote a book —?"

"I know who you mean," said the old man, smiling. "Was his name 'Kep' something?"

"Kephart," said the lieutenant.

"Yep. I knowed him," said the old man. The vessel's nose was swinging sluggishly to starboard and off-course. He spun the wheel to port and little by little she began to turn.

"They was a man named Bud Lowe who used to go everywhere with him. You remember a picture in the book of a mountaineer a-carryin' a big log? Well, that log was hollow"—the old man laughed, "an' the fellow a-holdin' it was Bud. I knowed him." The old man chuckled, his mind full of the past.

"If it hadn't been for that artheritis I reckon I'd still be there," he went on after a pause. "I had an orchard up near Elkmont, but my legs go to hurtin' me so an' the doctor said to git out in the sun an' the open air an' on the water if I could, so I went to sea."

The lieutenant looked about him. As far as the eye could reach was the vast emptiness of sloshing water, blue-black, with an occasional feather of foam where the wind whipped the top of a roller into frith. The engine's puffing was soft like a sigh, and the heavily laden ship wallowed on and on across the trackless waste.

"'So and no otherwise, hillmen prefer their hills,'" he quoted.

"What was that?" said the old man glancing at him. "I didn't catch it."

"I was just sort of thinking out loud." said the lieutenant. He turned away and stepped down out of the wheelhouse.

"I think I'll take a bearing," he said. "It looks like the sun might come out."

The Psalmist

"I will lift up mine eyes unto the hills," said the lieutenant softly.

"Sounds like the Bible," said the first mate between his teeth. He was holding a pipe in his mouth and couldn't talk very well

"It is," said the lieutenant.

There was a period of silence. The night had risen like dark vapor from the face of the deep to fill the cooling air. Only a few clouds in the west still showed the last luminous echoes of the buried sun, and in the east, Rigel, Capella, Aldebaran and bright Sirius had lit their tiny trembling lamps. The foam churned up by the blunt, thrusting prow of the plodding ship swept past below the wing of the flying bridge where the lieutenant leaned on the rail, gazing down at the carded white of the foam where the fitful glow of the phosphorous came and went in the black water like aquatic fireflies.

"That psalmist was a great man, I think," the lieutenant resumed. "He knew the earth and he knew the sea. I think he would have liked a place where I used to go."

He paused again, collecting the threads that went to the making of the colorful tapestry woven by his memory.

"It was fully 10 years ago that I was there last," he said. He spoke softly, easily, as though the speaking relieved him in some way. "We went there, my brothers and I, every year for three of four summers. It was in the Cherokee National Forest in the lower part of the Great Smokies, along the Tennessee-North Carolina line. We drove up in the Green Elephant, my 'A' model Ford roadster onto which we built a sort of temporary truck body, just for the occasion. I remember the last trip particularly well.

"It was in July or August, and the heat in the lowlands was terrific. There is a red heat to midsummer at home that somehow seems even more awful than the drenching heavy heat of the islands out here. We decided to go one day, and the next we were on our way, the poor Elephant fairly staggering under the overload that was stowed, stacked, and lashed aboard. We went up through Benton, that rude mountain village of violence and sudden death that is one of the last strongholds of pioneer naivete and direct action—on up the valley to Madisonville, across through Strawberry Plains to the outpost town of Tellico Plains.

"It was a spare, lean village, of gaunt dust-stained buildings, its only street unpaved. The whole settlement seemed sluggish and drugged, as though fallen under some hypnotic spell cast over it by the great green mountains, in whose shadows it lay. It was a place of hitching posts and dusty shade trees, where drowsy horses nodded, of dust-dim, fly-specked windows, of the cool dank interior of country stores with their bins and barrels of potatoes, apples and stale cakes, their cheap shoes, fishing lines and tobacco, their hardware, overalls, wide-brimmed, floppy straw hats and bolts of cloth, and all the cheap nostalgic smells that go to make such a place. We paused to buy last-minute supplies, including 50 pounds of ice, and then about 2:30 in the afternoon, we shook the dust of Tellico Plains off our wheels, crossed the rock-torn, rushing waters of the Tellico River, passed under the rustic arch of the gateway into the Cherokee National Forest, and were lost to civilization.

"The road follows the river. It has no alternative. Mile after mile it winds along beside the curving stream-bed, past pine thickets and steep leaning rocks, across narrow, flimsy-boarded bridges, now almost level with the cold green water, now suspended half-up a dizzy bluff over-hanging the swift-running river below. For 11 miles we drove—then, as we rounded a sharp turn in the narrow road, we heard the thunder of our welcome. A little way, and we crossed Bald River Falls. The thundering falls lay to our right, a cloud of silver spray building castles of misty haunting splendor in the blue air. Below the falls, Bald River sweeps into Tellico, and the two are merged into one.

"A quarter of a mile up the road we reached journey's end. To our left and below the road, set on a small level tableland that was only slightly above the stream, was our cabin. We wound down the steep rocky roadway leading in, and stopped. We were silent for a moment, hearing the green stillness of the spot, the only sound the liquid music of the hurrying stream. But it was mid-afternoon and already the sun was disappearing behind the steep forested hill across the stream to the west, and there was work to be done.

"First of all, we inspected the cabin. It was a long low building of stout pine logs. At the eaves it could not have been more than five and a half feet above the bare earth on which it stood, while at the ridgepole, it was about seven. There was the one long room with a table of hewn logs, a stone-masonry fireplace, and four tiny windows—and then, just off the main room at one end, was the little kitchen, with washstand, kerosene stove and small icebox.

"As usual, the place was filthy. The lock had been broken off the door, and there was a litter of cans and papers scattered about. We fell to work, three of us inside cleaning the cabin, the fourth cleaning the grounds outside. By the beginning of dusk, we had it cleaned, our stores and supplies stowed away, and the evening meal begun.

"Night falls swiftly in the deep mountain coves, and by the time we were done with supper, it was pitch dark. The kerosene lamp that swung from the roof tree over the table cast its warm golden light all through the room. The dank chill of the night air crept in through the door and the windows, and after we had scoured the dishes, we were glad to unfurl the cots, wrap up in a blanket, and fall asleep.

"We awoke to see the sun 'flatter the mountain-tops with sovereign eye, kissing with golden face the meadows green.' Not for several hours yet would it rise high enough to touch our shadowed retreat. So we breakfasted, cleaned up, and by the time the first spears of sunlight were splintering on the cold green waters of the little river, we were in swimming trunks in the stream, breasting the surging power of the current as we scrambled desperately from rock to rock.

"There was a great stone that stood squarely in the center of the stream, where we would lie for hours on end. It had been worn smooth by the waters of uncounted floods, the invisible drip of untold time. It stood there calm, serene and warm in the sun's rays. There we would lie all day, talking and dreaming, rousing occasionally to splash and play in the tugging water, or wandering off up or down stream with a fly rod to try to lure a strike from one of the small rainbow trout whose silver tensile strength was match enough for those cold, swift-running waters.

"The days blossomed and fell, one by one, into the silent pool of the past. They were like magic fruit that blooms in the morning, grows in the noon, and ripens and is plucked by evening. Some days we would read. Especially can I remember reading one book that I had taken with me to review for *The Times*. It was a thick, blue-bound volume titled "Mistress of Mistresses" by a man named E. R. Eddison, and was one of the most satisfying books I ever read. It was concerned with the after-world to which the great spirits of the earth go upon death, and with the intrigue and romance of that fabulous place. Then, too, at times we would write. I well remember how macabre and violent were some of the tales I wrote sitting in the dappling shade of the overbending trees outside the door of the cabin. And I can see so well the others: Bob, his dark curly hair crowning his finely modeled head, his handsome face cloudy with the dreams of youth, his sun-tanned body supple, well-muscled; and Si, he of the towering height, long, angular, silently puttering with bits of mechanical apparatus, a clock, the kerosene stove— his brown eyes shining, his strong teeth incredibly white against the bronze of his face, his full red lips; and David— the youngest—the

Benjamin of the family—lean-flanked and adolescent, his chiseled features proud, clean-carved and lovely with that proud beauty that was so much like our mother as to almost take the breath away.

"So we lazed through the golden days, occasionally driving down the narrow, winding dusty road to Tellico Plains for supplies and the mail. And it was as though it were springtime, and life spread out before us as fair, as promising as the fields and hills and valleys of April. There was no hooded bitterness, no shadow of the darkness ahead that would toss one of us aside with a medical discharge from the Navy, transplant two of us to the Orient, at the opposite end of the earth from home, and lay the youngest by the heels to sleep beneath the sod of the American Cemetery at Cambridge."

The lieutenant paused, and at that moment he looked older than he was.

"I remember the last night. All afternoon dark clouds had gathered about the mountain tops, swirling lower and lower. Occasionally above the tumult of the stream, we could hear the long echoing roll of thunder, as though great trunks were being tumbled downstairs in heaven. At last just before supper, the rains came.

"It was a wild night. The storm lashed at our snug little cabin. The rain was heavy on the roof. The cold breath of the storm stole in through cracks and crevices, and we lit the fire in the stone fireplace and it burned yellow and blue and red, the cheery flames singing a breathless song. The room was ruddy with lamplight, and we laughed and sang as the black wind and the drenching rain hurled themselves against roof and wall and ebony-mirrored window-panes and the heavy oak of our stout door.

"At last we were tired. The rain had settled to a thin monotone on the roof. We went to sleep, knowing that man has within him a spark of divinity, and that we were favored of the gods."

There was silence. Then the mate spoke.

"I've never seen mountains like that," he replied.

"The psalmist had," said the lieutenant.

Bell Buckle Spring

"It's a long way," said the lieutenant,
    leaning on the taff-rail
and looking out over the swell of the waves
    " a long way across these irregular furrows
of sloshing blue water,
    across the tropical green of islands,
across the hot white sand, the mountains,
    lying still as great carved jade cats under the sun—
back to the rolling green hill country
    of Bell Buckle, Tennessee, where I went to prep school."

He was silent a moment.
    The sea was a succession of mountains and valleys
of wind-wrinkled water,
    and white flowers of foam bloomed on the mountaintops.
"I remember," he went on—
    "I remember the golden haze of September afternoons,
the dust rising from the road
    as a T-model rattled by on its way to town.
I remember the brown of November,
    with dead leaves glutting the grounds,
the sharp needle of frost
    pricking out of the grey north,
the red-glowing belly of the stove
    in the Junior room,
and the early dusk that filled the cold air with blue mist
    thru which the stars bent down their pale and silver light
to touch a boy's heart with sadness
    for things gone and not to come again.

"I remember the winter—
    the frozen water in the washpan,
the snowflakes dancing in the lead-colored air,
    the earth frost-hard and stubborn,

and the unexpected holiday when the first snow fell to stick.
But most of all I remember the springtime.

"From my room on the second floor of the Burke House—
that room that was over the kitchen
and on a wing of the house that was called 'the caboose'
because it gave the impression
of having been tagged on at the end
as sort of an afterthought—
I had a magnificent view of the surrounding country.
The Burke House, a rambling, steep-sided,
ungainly and drab frame edifice of ancient vintage
and generally dilapidated condition,
was set atop a long swelling hill
that rose gradually from a creek to the northward,
and fell away into the graceful hills and hollows
of Pickens Pasture to the east, and south,
while to the west lay the school grounds.
Spring put on her loveliest guise for us of the Burke House
as though to compensate for the drabness of our domicile.

"There was a pear tree in the little hollow
that lay 'twixt us and the school,
and in April it was a foamy mass
of white sweet blossoms.
The sun, sweeping from south to north declination,
touched the hills and dales of Pickens Pasture
with its orange-golden fire
and lit the green flame of the grass
that spread over the rolling meadows
as far as the eager eye could follow.
There were dogwoods in the grove of trees
near and about where the library now stands,
and their fragile, scentless white blossoms
burned on the pale blue air
as sweetly as the choiring of the birds
that only a week before had been far south,
and now were come again to stir the hearts
of school boys and girls
and old men and women and all,
indeed, save the crafty, cunning and purely mercenary,

who cared not a fig
    for such vapid and intangible pleasures.

"Of a Monday afternoon—
    that being our holiday instead of Saturday—
we would leave the house
    and walk down the long hill away from town,
crossing the shallow creek
    on the dusty-timbered bridge,
then as the road bent to the left
    toward the old toll gate and Beech Grove,
we would turn right down a grassy lane
    that wound along beside the small, clear-voiced stream.
On either hand the ghosts of last year's cornfields
    rattled their faded tatters on the sweet blowing air,
and new grass was lush and green
    among the ancient rows.
Once in that lane
    we found three baby rabbits,
small grey-brown creatures with pinkish ears,
    crouched in the cool of the grass.
We picked them up gently,
    and they trembled in our hands,
and fleas jumped off them onto us and bit us,
    and we put the rabbits down again
and watched them disappear
    into the sanctuary of the deep grass.

"On and on we would wander,
    talking, throwing rocks,
touched by the warmth of the April sun.
    On the hills was the glow of redbud in bloom
and the snow of dogwoods
    and always the deep somber note of the evergreens,
the cedars that stood whispering to each other
    among the grey boney rocks
of the limestone hillsides.
            Then we would climb over an old wall—
one of those walls made of stones
    merely laid on top each other,
with no mortar or cement between—
    feeling the grey rain-worn stones warm to the touch,

and we would walk across the long swelling undulance
    of Pickens Pasture.
The earth was springy underfoot—
    the grass short-clipped by the sheep
that dotted the rolling expanse of the pasture.
    As we passed the sheep,
they would lift their heads
    and gaze after us with their strange, gentle eyes, and bleat,
and they were usually dirty,
    their wool full of cockleburrs and filth
hanging stringily from them.
After a time we would come to a creek
that ran thru the pasture.
    The creek had cut its bed deep across the meadow
and it was eight of ten feet down
    from the grassy floor of the meadow to the clear cold water
that sparkled and splashed ins musical way
    along over roots and stones,
now running loud and shallow, now deep and still.
    Following the meandering of the stream
we would come in late afternoon
    to where the pasture was bounded
on the west and south by the railroad.
    And there we would stop.

"The track lay neat,
    its shining rails, its grey crushed limestone ballast
curving away into the blue-green distance.
    There was a steely stillness about that track
that gripped the heart of a boy,
    even on a spring afternoon
when one's dreams are wild and colorful
    and full of extravagant loveliness and enchantment
and a wordless swelling cry toward fulfillment.
    The blue of the sky deepened as dusk approached,
and in the stillness we could hear
    the distant lowing of cattle anxious for the milking
and the dim barking of dogs.
    We would touch one of the rails
and it was cold and heavy.
    And so we would wait until at last we felt it—

the dim prescience of something that came
   and was unknown and afar off—
the distant ominous roar—
   and then the faint wind-borne whistle.
And soon, far down the distant line of the track
   there was a black speck that drew near and nearer,
and finally it was a locomotive,
   rocking from side to side as it raced toward us,
its smoke blown back like black wind-torn hair.
   And we saw the white of its whistle steam.
And then we heard its screaming and it cried to us,
   and again, and again, and its cry was one of anguish
and sorrow and courage and bright hope,
   of departure and loss—
and of the coming again.
   Then it was upon us, and turned the curve
by the corner of the pasture,
   its tall drivers high and flashing
like the knees of a strong runner,
   its pistons hitting fast
like the arms of a powerful and tireless fighter.
   The noise of its passing
shook the countryside like thunder,
   and our hearts trembled and bowed down
before its majesty and flying strength.
   And its engineer
leaned on the armrest of the cab window,
   his left hand loosely gripping the throttle,
and waved his gloved right hand and smiled,
   his goggled face hawk-like and clean and strong
as the stride of the great running iron horse he handled.
   Then there was the thunder of the coaches sweeping past,
and then they were gone,
   and the train and the clickety-clack
of its wheels dwindled into the distance,
   and the calm and the stillness of the country landscape
flowed back again and it was time to go home.

"So back over the hills and hollows we would walk—
   going straight this time, not following
the wanderings of the meadow brook.
   We were quiet, our hearts caught

39

in the spell of the train.
     To the west the sun was setting
in a cloud castle with high rose-colored walls,
     and the sky beyond was a luminous blue
more beautiful than anything in the world.

"To the east, day had deepened into dusk.
     A single planet shone pale
in the vast emptiness of the darkening air.
     Then we reached a fence and climbed it—
and we were almost back to the house."

The lieutenant was silent,
     not seeing the small blue flying fish
that skimmed the water—
     not seeing anything, indeed, that was at hand.

"It was spring and was a long time ago," he said—
     "but it is still good."

Kings Cross—Sydney

It was a fair morning. I could sense it as soon as I awoke. During the night we had slipped in through the headlands and dropped anchor, and as I came on deck in the blue and gold of post-dawn, I saw a wondrous sight.

The harbor was full of ship—battle-gray warships with iron names: The King George V, The Illustrious, The Black Prince; lean, tired destroyers, oil-streaked, looking like wolfhounds after a run; battered, rusty cargo vessels, and all manner of small harbor craft.

On the good green earth that locked in the harbor on every hand were the geometric designs of the city: the angle and still flight of buildings that soared steep and white into the sun-stroked blue of the immense and brooding sky, and were dimly, haunting beautiful in the blue-blurred distance. Gulls scribed their curving flight upon the air, their feathers white as snow save for the black bars on their wings. The sunlight fell in a pale golden shower, having, withal, a tender warmth that flushed the face and the heart, and as we moved into the inner harbor passing beneath the mighty span of the webbed high-arching bridge, we felt the slight chill of the shadow of the bridge, and our hearts were constricted by sorrow and exultation for the wonder and the loneliness of man. And there was before us and within us the vision of that city, and it was like a dream, bright with every beautiful color, and at the center of the dream was one fairer than Helen, whose long white limbs were sown with ruddy fire, and were ecstasy and devotion. Within the fragrant forest of her hair was sanctuary, and in her sweet drowning love lay the two ultimate treasures: forgetfulness and discovery. Surely we felt—surely here would be that Golden One—Mistress of Mistresses—she whose golden charms would lend enchantment to all the world so that henceforward everything we touched would turn to gold, and all the words unspoken, the dreams forgotten, the desires never quite attained, would spring into existence!

As we came, we tasted the air, sweet, heavy with the land smell, golden orange with the sun. And we made fast to the dock and stepped ashore, and the earth was strong underfoot, and we knew the certainty of our destiny and that it was good.

There was much to be seen, to be felt.

The walk up the hill in the sunlight. The trams full of people, the broad streets and the sidewalks. The bake shops, redolent of the yeasty warm fragrance of baking bread. The pubs with their dark-colored swinging doors and the gush of beer-smell that poured forth. The buildings, lifting clean and strong into the air, the sun casting its web of golden swarming light upon the time-worn walls and roofs, overlaying the dirt and grime with its bright lacquer.

At the top of the hill was the park—the green of the grass and the shrubs. People were sitting on little iron benches in the park, dreaming placid and open-eyed in the sunlight. Fat pigeons fluttered in the thin blue air or waddled about importantly, burbling to each other, their heads bobbing with every step they took.

Again I felt in my throat the fullness—my chest was filled to bursting with the surging joy of discovery—the rediscovery of the goodness of cities, of the swarms of people thronging the streets, the friendly faces, the interested eyes—all for me, the bronzed, open-collared, in faded khaki pants and a worn jacket and a cap the gold of which was tarnished a dull green by the salt air of the wind-blown seas. I was intoxicated by the smell of gasoline, the clangor of tram bells, the fresh color of shop windows, the glorious beauty of girls and the undulance of their walk, the shape of a profile, the curve of an eyebrow, the promise of a smile—and all, all printed strong and plain against the background of the roaring traffic, streaked across by the shrill stabbing whistle, silver-sharp, of a policeman.

It was good. It was all good. But the best part was this: going into a fruit shop and tasting the rich, full-bodied bouquet of the place, filled as it was with the bright golden color of oranges, the delicate yellow of pears and bananas and lemons, the shining scarlet of luscious juicy-sweet apples, and every conceivable kind of fruit—even strawberries, wild and shy and pink as the breasts of young desire. And there were the milk bars, with the ice cream and chocolate syrup and creamy-cold malted milk. And from the door of a small cafe came the tantalizing, indescribable fragrance of a broiling steak—that good rich smell, full of the flavor of hot butter with a touch of onion, so that the nose must needs wrinkle and the mouth water.

Beside these things, there were the books in the bookshop windows, friendly and warm and beckoning—the leather shops, full of the sharp, heart-stinging smell of good leather—the arcades, lined with stalls and full of milling, mobbing people—and all the other million sights and sounds and smells of a great city.

The golden afternoon sank into dusk. Away to the West in lovely distant isolation was smudged the faint long line of the Blue Mountains. The air chilled, for it was winter—albeit more like late fall—and as twilight thickened into darkness, the lights began to wink on, and all across the maze of streets and buildings, of alleys and parks and intricate fabrications that begirdle and form a metropolis, it was as though stars had been sown broadcast, and they shone warm and luminous in the crisp air.

It was full of glory that night to walk the streets, hearing the clatter of heels on the pavement, the gay chatter, the laughter—and always and ever the paper boys crying their wares into the cold blowing darkness, their hoarse jargon that same wordless brave melancholy cry as all over the world—(and I remembered the street corner in Chicago, deep-lost in a canyon of night-drowned buildings, with the snow swirling down thick and soft and cold, and that same nameless crying). And papers are tuppence.

You are a drop in the stream of humanity, and you are carried along in the slow, thick current with the good and the bad, the generous and the stingy, the doers and the refrainers, the strong and the weak. And ever and ever again you see a face that has strength and beauty, and your heart cries: "There! There! That one—that must be—!" And the face disappears, is swallowed up in the dark stream and is gone, and you know that never again will that same strong beauty flash upon the retina of your eye—and it was lost before it was found—and you are overwhelmed by a wave of loneliness and despair, because there is so little time, so little time, and so much love that is wasted or never found.

And yet again, on another night, in a flash, in the twinkling of an eye, the mood changed, and you saw the city illumined with the brilliance and the bitter artificiality that is the mark of all great cities. There is a curious thing about this artificiality. It is at first glance so good, so beautiful—until you see, as by the flicker of lightning, that it is in reality like the face of a woman wearing heavy makeup, and you see the hard lines, the falsity of the eyebrows, the thin bitter line of the true mouth beneath the rich sensuous one that was painted on, and the black selfishness and sense of loss and futility in the mascaraed eyes. There is no love there—none of the warmth, the deep brooding affection and tenderness of lamplight flowing through the half-closed eyes of village windows, or of firelight flickering on the rude rafters of a cottage in the fresh countryside, where the dark wind breathes across the fields, sweet with fresh dew and the trailing perfume of honeysuckle, and the moon climbs out of the dark thickets of the East and hangs against the black curtain of the night like a huge balloon, as ruddy-orange as a smoked cheese.

In the harlot city even the sounds become harsh and shallow: the whine of the beggar, the slam of a car door, the grinding of gears, the distant thumping dissonance of a cheap band playing "Rum and Coca Cola." The lanes and alleys are choked with shadows, the night air is cold and damp, and you thrust your hands deeper into your pockets to keep them warm, and you think of Kings Cross.

Kings Cross . . . on top of the hill, where five streets run together, and the slums of Woollamalloo meet the uptown of King and Williams. The Greenwich Village of the Land Down Under. The hot spots and the floozies are so thick that you have to wade through them. Where the air sparkles with the cold brilliance of perfume, and yawns with the warm fragrance of a woman's body . . . where love is cheap, and where the corpse of bartered love stares unwinking through a smudged window-pane into the emptiness of an unstarred sky. There is the svelte night-club and the unemotional sobbing of saxophones and the idiot pounding of a drum, and the high reedy giggle of a clarinet—and sparkling wine (instead of champagne) at a pound a fifth, and the mascaraed girls saying, "Darling, please give me a cigarette," and "Have you a match?" . . . and lots of the girls have false teeth (that gleam at you in your dreams out of the watery prism of a glass tumbler) and they all have painted hollow smiles, and the bald-headed major with three children on the other side of the world laughs drunkenly and lurches against a table, and the heavy-lidded lieutenant kisses a peroxide blonde and shivers and calls for the bill, and the headwaiter is impeccable in tails and black-and-white etiquette, and you say, "Christ, where are the stars?"

Kings Cross. I remember a taxi and a sailor and his tart, and he got out and she rode on with me and we talked. She said, "There are too many girls here" and coughed. Then said, "Have you a cigarette?" and coughed again, and the lights were burning bitter and cheap in the curdled darkness.

Then there was a girl—what was her name? Surely I haven't forgotten! And she had lupa hair tumbling in dark cascade to her shoulders and she was young and passionately silly and a phrase fell into my mind and struck a bell-like note, and it kept ringing on and on. It was the title of a book I had once heard of but had never read "Conrad In Quest of His Youth." And I was busy listening with half my head to small talk and trying to think of something to say, but everything I started to say was trite and trivial (like what was being said) and I hesitated to say it, and by the time I decided to quit hesitating it was too late—they were talking about something else. And with the other half of my head I was thinking that somewhere there was a person who was lovely and deep and understanding and deliciously sensitive and responsive—and I had known her and she was real and not a dream—and how damned cheap this all was. There was a gulf between me and the rest of the party—a gulf that even alcohol couldn't bridge. But we had dinner and danced and drank and I wanted to talk—but talk, real talk, is a revelation, and I felt indecent about it, like going swimming naked where it isn't done, so I didn't. But the others talked.

The dark-haired girl drank too much, and when we left, shortly after midnight, she was drunk and decided she wanted a cat and wandered up and down the alleyways near the Cross calling "pussy-pussy—here pussy!" and insulting all the limey sailors and marines that passed by singing the Yank's Marine Song. The last train had run and the cabs were off the streets for the night. We had to walk a hell of a distance down Williams Street and up a hill and through Hyde Park to Elizabeth. Finally an owl tram came by and she caught it and I let the other couple take her home and went off down the street whistling that wistful lilting melody of a doomed people called "Lili Marlene"—and I felt like I had thrown up a whale, or been thrown up by one.

It was deep night. The stars were white splintered fragments in the dark-vaulted heavens, and the shadow-somber streets were lonely and cold. As I walked along hearing the hollow ring of my boot heels on the sidewalk (which they called the footpath) I wondered how many sons of men were abroad in the midnight, walking the desolate dim streets with their hearts full of the anguish and the stale flat taste of Kings Cross.

Oh—Sydney is a good town. There's the Zoo and the Botanical Gardens and Hyde Park. There are shops and friendly people and—sometimes good food. There is one quiet luxurious place hidden down an alley that leads off a crooked lane—a place of deep carpets and indirect lighting and fresh white double-thick table linen and exquisitely flavored French food, and there are fresh rosebuds on each tiny table and the dark wine bottles shine gently, and the wine is like a jewel in the crystal goblet—the pale gold of topaz or the dark gleaming red of ruby—and the place is called The Hermitage, and is owned by the Food and Wine Society. Then there are bookstores, though the shelves are poorly stocked on account of the war, and the native sons are not very good writers—at least the ones I noted.

The climate is much like that of New Orleans. There are scarlet poinsettias and camellias and cape jasmine and azaleas. And as in the Crescent City, the shops and stores have marquees extending out over the footpaths.

When it rains, the rain blows along the street and you can hear it rattling on the tin marquee and there is a dank chill everywhere, but you can go in and have hot tea (with lemon in it if you insist) and crumpets, and it warms you up.

When the sun is shining, the wind blows cool and blue-green and the sunlight pours upon you its warmth and gentle color and your heart tugs at its moorings and you look into every face with joy and love and compassion.

But in the evening when the sun has set, dusk rises like slow smoke to fill the cold air with darkening blue, and as the stars burn through, one's heart is pricked with melancholy and there comes again the vision—the dream of love that is magic and cannot be found—the depthless beauty of unattainable desire that is at once, the life—and death—or should I say the triumph— defeat?—of Kings Cross.

The Band Played On—Brisbane

It was dawn—what has been called day-spring.

The water in the bay was a rich purplish blue. The sun was low in the East, and the air was full of its flat golden light. A chilly wind blew in from the sea, and the mangrove swamps at the mouth of the river were blurred by the wind. Their darker green stood out sharp and strong against the paler aqua of the flatland beyond. Gulls were wheeling in the sweet morning air. They were white with black markings on their wing tips, and when they came near you could see that their feet and legs were red. The color and the sweetness of the morning were like magic.

As our ship moved up the river behind the bull-shouldered little tug, the land on either hand changed. After the swamps came pasture land that flowed away, green and sun-gilt, the cattle standing in little groups, calm, flicking their tails, their shadows falling long and blue across the dewy grass. In the distance were the barns, red-roofed and almost lost in the mistiness of the morning air that lent a dimness and unreality to the scene.

Then from behind the little hills the town emerged.

It was built upon and around the hills, and as far as the eye could follow were the red roofs of the houses, the white walls, blue-splashed with shadow, the color of gardens where poinsettias burned cool and crimson and where flame trees held aloft the crimson of their flower-flambeaux, and flowers bloomed in a riot of colors.

Many of the houses were built along the very edge of the blue-brown river, the carefully mown lawns dipping their emerald edges daintily into the water, the neatly clipped hedges glittering with dew. The houses were of stucco, or of brick, or of wood and were clean, fresh-painted, and marvelously beautiful in the golden sunlight. Then, there ahead was the long surging leap of a single-span bridge, frozen in mid-air, and strongly wrought against the soft blue of the sky. Its iron webbing was clean, sharp and triumphantly secure. And the giant white concrete towers that held the span ends were rosy and unbelievably lovely in the swarming sunlight.

After passing under the bridge, we tied up at the Howard Smith

Docks. Leaning on the rail of the flying bridge, I stared down into the water, mesmerized by the tender and dream-like beauty of the morning. The river was full of clumps of hyacinths—the knotted green of the tubers, the floating tendrils, drifting sluggishly down to the sea.

I was as one bemused, and watched with idle impersonal eyes the little drama of the making fast—the throwing of the heaving line, the hauling in of the heavy hawsers, the warping in to the dock that marks the return to earth of those who have been part of the sea—part of the spindrift, the gentle silver lamp of the morning star, the lift and fall of the long shouldering swell.

With an effort I roused myself. Going below, I gathered up the mail for posting and, leaving the ship, I quitted the dock by way of the Customs Gate and set out for the Naval Station where I knew I would find a Fleet Post Office.

It was good to set foot upon the solid earth, to feel the hardness of the dark blue asphalt underfoot, the grimy gray of concrete, and to see the myriad forms and faces of men and women, each with their own history and hopes.

Upon inquiry I was told to catch a New Farms Wharf tram and to get off at Stop 15. I caught the first tram rumbling by that had the words "New Farm" on it, told the conductor I wanted to get off at Stop 15, and relaxed to enjoy the ride.

It was a picturesque one, through a small suburban shopping district, then out through the residential district. The houses were neat and clean, and there was a profusion of flowers. It seemed so strange: here it was winter, as I knew the Aussie months of the year, yet the sun was so warm, so golden . . . and—strangest of all—it was winter in June! The sun was far in the north, and the shadows wove their dark counterpoint even at noon.

On and on we went. Then, just as we pulled up by a park, the conductor said to me, "Where was it that you wanted to get off?"

"Stop 15" I said.

"Oh—I'm sorry," he said, "We passed that a good way back. But—we'll bring you back again. Where were you going?"

"To the Naval Station," I replied.

He glanced about.

"Get off here," he said quickly—"Go through the park that way (indicating) and you'll be there . You are on the wrong car. You wanted New Farms Wharf—and this is New Farms Park!"

I thanked him and scrambled off the tram, just as it moved on.

The walk through the park was even more beautiful than the ride up the river. It was a place of rose bushes—perhaps you would even call them rose trees. There were huge bushes, dripping with dew and covered with red or pink or yellow or white roses in all stages of bloom. Against the vivid emerald of the well-trimmed lawn and soft green of the willows and jacarandas, the fresh color of the roses was symphonically perfect. Everything was dew-sparkling, and the fragrance of the roses stabbed me with almost unbearable sweetness. The gardeners were digging a new rose bed as I went by, and the newly turned earth was chill and dark, and its loamy smell, dark and secret and full of the mystery of earth and death, made a fugue of rare and haunting loveliness. Birds sang in the nodding willows, and on a battered wooden bench in the full-gold splendor of the sunlight dozed an ancient, his gnarled old hands clutching a walking stick. My heart was suddenly chilled by the realization that time was pouring out in that stream of sunlight—that for all the beauty and the color of life, there was the ever-constricting noose of mortality and mutation, and that the dark earth waited patiently.

I arrived at the Naval Station and found that there was mail. They gave me a car and a driver from the motor pool and I went back to the ship. I, myself, had 37 letters, and Nick and I sat in my cabin tearing ends off envelopes and devouring the words inside until I was seized by literary indigestion and quit, left the ship, and walked through the grimy streets of the city searching for I knew not what—and, of course, never finding it.

Brisbone is a strange city. Although it had a population of nearly half a million, it was withal, but a loose, disjointed small town—or series of small towns lumped into one. The shops and streets were old-fashioned and inadequate. To be in that city was like waking up to find that the present was just a dream, and that you were really living 25 years earlier. The dingy shops, the grimy sidewalks, the dignified and ridiculous advertisements—everything was as it had been a quarter of a century before in the small towns of the United States. Even the automobiles were ancient. I saw 1918 Buicks, 1920 Dodges, 1924 Fords, Willis Knights, Stearns—even an antique Essex, and others whose names have long since vanished, consumed by the slow burning of time. Yet, in this very old-fashiondness, there was a goodness, a heady delight such as is to be found in a venerable wine whose color and bouquet has become more enjoyable with the passage of the years.

And if the city were of a lost age, its inhabitants were equally so. They were sturdy and plain, full of honest interest and friendliness. I will never forget them.

Captain (was it Angus?) Firth, the older brother of our first mate, was a stalwart, heavy-handed man of quiet dignity and strength who gave an appearance of stoic calm and unemotionalism. But beneath this exterior was a creature of fire and ice. He was a product of the sailing ships, having served as a cadet, mate, and master. Indeed, he was chief officer of that magnificent full-rigged ship, The Mount Stewart, when Colin (our first mate) shipped aboard her as a cadet.

Captain Firth loved the sea and those who loved the sea. He pressed upon me a book by William McFee, and held me spellbound with his tales of such high adventure and gaudy romance that I ended up quite drunken on the conversation, and staggered back to my ship to dream of snowy-winged clippers and huge albatross and ear-ringed pirates in red pantaloons and the ruddy blurt of lamplight shining on pieces of eight.

I remember particularly his saying that the mast of The Mount Stewart was originally 210 feet high—as tall as a 20-story building!

On Sunday—that being our second day there—I went to church with a shipmate, Win Frecker—whose nickname was Rocky. We left the docks and climbed the crooked old streets to the top of the hill, the site of St. Johns Cathedral. It was a sonnet in stone, that cathedral, if I ever saw one. Apparently it had been built with the thought that it might be enlarged at some later date, thereby completing a larger original plan, but its balance and execution could not be improved. The green lawns, the delicate coloring of its soaring stone turrets that soared into the steep blue heights of the morning air—all was a power and glory that were deeply moving. We stood in the shadow of its walls, our hearts witched by the scene: the black and white vestments of the priests and deacons—the scarlet cassocks of the acolytes—the sunlight touching the green grass with its fire—the trembling blue of the shadows; and after we went in, there was the gentle gloom of the cool, lofty-ceiled nave, the a-sexual voices of the boys choir, the simple dignity, solemn beauty, and flowing poetry of the service of morning prayer.

When we stood to sing "God Save The King," and I saw the British flag hung by the lectern, and standing shoulder to shoulder beside it, the red and white stripes and the starry field of our own flag, I felt the tears rush to my eyes. My spirit was enchanted by that holy place, and—little though I knew or understood—I felt the goodness of life and of God flow cool and cleansing through my very bones and marrow.

The service over, we left and walked back to the ship, knowing we were richer than before.

That afternoon, having met the skipper and his cousin, Len—an ex-RAF chap - I went to the Botanical Gardens with them.

As we entered the Garden gates, we were asked if we would make a donation to the band which would play a concert that afternoon. We did—and then passed on inside.

The footpath we followed ran along the grassy banks of the river. There were small white yachts in the river and their reflections shone in the mirroring water. Across the river were steep cliffs of salmon-colored rock washed by the sunlight. As we walked on, the path led away from the water and up the hill among flowering shrubs. On the top of the hill was a great banyan tree, its thick smooth-barked branches stretching in all directions, the trailing twigs of its outspread arms yearning down toward the earth (for it is the peculiarity of that tree that its branches turn earthward and become rooted in the ground, and in a sense, are separate trees).

On over the hill we went, down past the Wallaby Corral, the bird-houses where peacocks strutted in all their iridescent finery, and a ludicrous white pelican waddled about like a slightly disreputable and pot-bellied old man, the monkey cages, and the crowd on the lawn where "Captain the Wonder Dog," a German shepherd, was going through his mute and inglorious performance beneath the lashing tongue of his trainer—and so we came at last to the bandstand.

The band was playing and the scene was an idyllic one: the green undulations of the turfy hill, the classic simplicity of the bottle trees and palms, the light of late afternoon falling like slow golden mist, the vivid red of the flame trees and the poinsettias. And the people! There were people of all ages and descriptions: old men and women with pale, cool eyes; children romping and playing in the grass, their faces and holiday clothing as bright and colorful as flowers; and young men and girls—the latter fresh-colored and lovely in clean bright gowns, their haunches beautifully curved, their stride eager yet cautious, their breasts proud but somehow afraid of the flame of love that smouldered in their loins ready to burst into fiery flower.

And the band played on.

After a bit the musicians stopped awhile, then, after catching their breath, began re-tuning their instruments. The air was full of furtive pipings and tootlings. Some of them stared loftily and moodily down from their pedestal on the bandstand, eyeing the assembled multitude with that vast and superior indifference that is peculiar to minor artists. The bandmaster stood up again, waved his arms, and again they began to play.

This time it was selections from Gilbert & Sullivan. The gay light music, full of bouncy rhythm, harmonized with the scene. The children skipped to its beat—the lovers swung their clasped hands to its rhythm—even the blue-uniformed young policeman in his white peaked helmet with chin strap, whirled his nightstick in time with the drumbeat. And my heart was filled with love and gratitude for the sweet beauty of that dying afternoon, that afternoon of a day so far from the mountains of my home, yet still a part of the surging heart of man that is—wherever found—the true home of everyone who is a part of mankind.

The sun sank lower, and finally, when it was hovering just above the horizon, we left. As we walked out through the gates of the Gardens, children were buying candied apples on sticks from an old man. Sixpence apiece, I believe they were. The laughter of the children was like prismed crystal balls tossed in the dusty-gold air. Dim and far away, the band played on—Strauss waltzes, it was now. And, from somewhere down the river, fogged by distance and almost unheard, came the long-drawn mournful lowing of a ship's whistle. The sound was soft yet ominous, for it spoke of departure, and the mortality of love, beauty, even of life itself. We walked back to the ship almost without speaking

Next morning we cast off and moved slowly down the river in the early sunlight, leaving the city to its magic drowsy dreams, the vision unbroken, remembering the light blue wing of the shadows upon the stones, the sun lacquering the worn and time-rubbed walls, the unspoiled colors of the Gardens, the merry music of the band, and the water hyacinths eddying slowly in the inexorable grip of the river that flowed without ceasing down, down to the sky-colored sea.

Getting the News

It was grey dawn when I woke. Within a minute and a half I was on the bridge—I was in no hurry.

The sea was calm, glassy . . . The last stars were paling in the lighting air . . . On the rim of the world the trembling colors of imminent dawn burned cool and fragile . . . The ships about us were like toys carved of ebony and set upon a green glass-topped table . . . They seemed scarcely to move.

I sat on the grey painted steps of a gun-tub, drinking the chill, sweet air, and watching the night sink into the sea like thin purple mist that floated down, gentle and sad out of the sky . . . Soon day would break . . . The tropic sun would leap from the blue-green water with a thunder of cascading molten gold, and the clangor of iron heat would begin. I wondered why it was that this dawn seemed so much lovelier—so much more poignant—than any I had ever seen.

Then I went below and shaved, and by that time it was broad daylight and the chow bell had rung and I went down to the saloon.

It was a bare room, with three—no, four—little tables for four persons each. A green-leathered seat stretched along the entire forward bulkhead, furnishing seats for one side of three of the tables, while on the other side were yellow oaken swivel chairs, two to a table. I sat down in one of the chairs beside the chief engineer—the most charmingly and innocently blasphemous and foul-tongued man I ever knew—and ordered oatmeal. I sat there drumming my fingers on the tablecloth, which was not very clean. Through the portholes in the forward bulkhead I could see the blue sky, full of the glittering gold of the sunlight. I could hear the muffled trembling vibration of the engines, the whine of electric fans, the abrupt, musical voice of a Japanese prisoner—an old man—on the hatch-cover outside talking to his three children. Then I heard something else.

The radio was on, and through the splutter and squawk of static, I heard a voice that I was sure was that of H. V. Kaltenborn, the great purist: the precise enunciation—the air of imparting profound, exciting and but-just-now-discovered knowledge—yes, it could be none other. And he seemed to be making a speech on the subject of Franklin

Roosevelt . . . What he was saying was very complimentary . . . I wondered if some trick were being played—if this were a flashback to pre-election days. But—no, Kaltenborn had not even supported the President, as I recalled. I turned to the chief.

"Sounds like Roosevelt must be dead—all those nice things Kaltenborn's saying about him."

"He is," said the purser, who was sitting at the next table. The purser wore horn-rimmed glasses and looked owlish. I didn't believe him. Then the first radio operator spoke up:

"Yes, he's dead. We heard it at 3:30 this morning."

I stopped breathing.

The voice on the radio crackled on.

"Dead? I said faintly. "Dead?"

They all nodded. Their mouths were full. Their jaws moved rhythmically as they chewed, solemn-eyed.

My oatmeal had come. I put butter and sugar and canned milk on it and began to eat.

"My God!" I said. "Truman is President. Willkie is dead. . . . It's bad. . . . . It's bad. . . ."

The oatmeal was like gray glue. Or perhaps it was just the way I felt. Suddenly the whole world within me—and the most important world is that within—had clouded, and rain was falling.

"Well," I said, "that's no good. . . . This is a hell of a time for that to happen."

I saw the picture of the man: his jutting chin, his smile, his angled cigarette holder, his great, heavy-shouldered body, so powerful, so unhelplessly helpless. . . . I remembered his silver-spooned past, his mellifluous voice, his sense of the dramatic—his fabled devotion to the cause of justice and fair dealing. . . . All the weaknesses, the mistakes, and on the other hand, the supple overwhelming strength of his personality, his idealism! Remembered the words about him—the bitter, suspicious words; the invective; the unreasoning adulation . . . and now he was done . . . dust.

I kept thinking how all across the world, men and women who were fighting, working, loving, sleeping, were getting the word. . . . Tired-faced men in tents and foxholes, on ships and winging through the vaulted sky; on busses and trains, beside parlor radios and stooping in the green and gold dawn to pick up the morning paper—all were getting the news. In Rangoon and Iloilo—in Guam and the Aleutians—in Russia, Germany, France, South America, and the wide, lonely, mystic and powerful plains and mountains and valleys of our America—the whole earth was hearing—and as they heard they stopped breathing and stared, unseeing, into space.

But what of the world? Who will hold the reins of steel to check and guide the stormy-breasted stallions of vengeance and despair, whose lashing hooves are thundering over the earth? The San Francisco conference: Who will speak for us?

"Thank God for Churchill," I said.

I couldn't eat anymore. So I got up, lifted my cap from its hook by the door and went out.

I went up the outside ladder, climbing steeply into the pale blue coolness of the morning sky. . . . A group of my men were standing in a little knot on the bridge.

"Is it true, lieutenant?" one said. They were quiet, trouble-eyed.

"Yes," I said. "It is true."

I looked aft.

Clean and gloriously beautiful, the red and white-striped ensign fluttered at half mast. There was something very living, very lovely and tender and proud about that flag. My eyes burned and my throat ached and I felt like a fool because I was afraid to try to talk.

Then I went down to Blaxton's cabin. He was the Army lieutenant.

He was asleep. I turned on the light, and he sat up drowsily.

"Get up G. L.," I said harshly. . . ."Roosevelt's dead."

Wake Up, World!

It was about 2200 and I was asleep on the boatdeck, but they woke me. "Wake up!" they said—"the war's over!"

I opened my eyes. We were anchored out beyond the reef, lost in the purple sea of the tropical night. Then, as I looked toward the shore, I saw a strange sight.

There were lights on, all up and down the beach. Great searchlights probed the night, carving white curves on the star-flecked darkness. Colored flares—green, yellow, red and white --squirted up like reversed comets and burst into sudden bright bloom, burning like slow falling stars as they parachuted down. Red streaks of anti-aircraft tracers arched into the sky.

By this time the ships had wakened, and guns began to speak all around us. A near-by Liberty cut loose with all its armament spouting at once—20-mm's thumping, and the big bow and stern guns crashing away, splintering the cool, dark night air. We could hear the hum of the shells winging skyward where they burst in splintering explosions of light, the faint "whoompf!" of the bursts falling slow and soft. Then, very far away, we heard a heavy thudding boom, followed by another and another and another. The concussion made our ship tremble, and the air shook with the vibrations of the projectiles' flight. It must have been a battlewagon, cutting loose with its 16-inchers. Flak began to fall near us. We heard it hitting the water, and got under cover.

"Hurray for our side," said the medical major, dispassionately. "I hope the bastards don't hit us."

It was hard to tell how I felt. I know I didn't feel like yelling or getting drunk. I was glad—but I felt like crying.

It was funny what I thought about, I guess. I thought first of all of home. I could see them. They were listening to the radio, and their eyes were bright with tears, and they couldn't talk for the hurt in their throats. I thought about the ones who couldn't celebrate because they were dead—or worse. (Did you ever watch a boy consciously go mad?) I thought of the big-shouldered man buried in the rose garden at Hyde Park—of Winnie the Indomitable, already repudiated by the people he saved—of little Ernie Pyle, who understood the G. I.'s war better than any—of the kids at home, awkward, adolescent, just growing into young manhood, whose lives had been snuffed out—and of the monstrous responsibility of America and Britain as creators of the atomic bomb.

Sobering thoughts.

In "Brave Men" Ernie Pyle said it best of all:

"The end of the war will be a gigantic relief, but it cannot be a matter of hilarity for most of us. Somehow it would seem sacrilegious to sing and dance when the great day comes—there are so many who can never sing and dance again. . . . For some, the war has already gone on too long. Our feelings have been wrung and drained; they cringe from the effort of coming alive again. Even the approach of the end seems to have brought little inner elation. It has brought only a tired sense of relief. We have won this war because our men are brave and because of many other things—because of Russia and England, and the passage of time, and the gift of nature's materials. We did not win it because destiny created us better than all other peoples. I hope that in victory we are more grateful than we are proud. I hope we can rejoice in victory—but humbly. The dead men would not want us to gloat. . . ."

That's how we feel.

The job is only begun. A world lost for six long years in a nightmare of death and destruction still rubs its eyes and blinks, uncomprehending.

Wake up, world! The war's over!

The Woman Named Tomorrow

Taking what is admittedly a distant view of the situation, the prospect of what we are to return to seems far from bright. Aside from the overwhelming gladness of being back with those we know and love, there is little to appeal to the heart that is weary with death and struggle.

Selfishness and materialism, which even before the war held far too powerful a place in our America, have even more firmly entrenched themselves. A civilization that saw its youth thrust into the fiery furnace of war—and quite logically melted down the gold of their slain hearts—turns to fresh fields.

Labor, apparently a bit intoxicated on the heady war wages, demands a thirty per cent increase. We wonder if they realize that war wage standards are necessarily higher than those of peace—that if increase is to be had, prices must mount, and inflation increase; and that the better thing is to try to hold wages where they are, and to get prices down—a device that is possible in a competitive economy such as the United States has.

It is the consensus of the overwhelming majority of the GI's that I happen to have talked with that the time has come for governmental regulation of labor. They are disturbingly impressed by the arrogant power of labor leadership. They say that reforms such as (a) a compulsory secret ballot for all union voting; (b) an abolition of the closed shop; (c) compulsory accounting to Government and union members by all unions, and (d) unions' responsibility under the antitrust laws, should be enacted. Many also favor the establishment of labor tribunals to hear and decide quarrels between management and labor. In the event labor lost the case, the workers would still be able to quit work—but not to strike (that is, retain any hold on their jobs and refuse to let others work there). If management lost, they could be compelled to obey by mandatory injunction.

Capital—perhaps because it has no alternative—seems to be in a more reasonable frame of mind. The recently announced proposal to break up the Aluminum Company of America into a number of competitive organizations sounds good. It indicates a trend away from the centralization of economic power. Most industry is faced with a terrific problem in readjusting to peacetime production and still retaining their labor—on a margin of profit that cannot compare with that of wartime conditions. The wiser industries are devoting much time and thought to giving labor more of a stake in the gamble. After all, the whole capitalist system is but a game of pitch and toss in which, in addition to blind chance, the potent factors of ability, ingenuity and industry are also of weight.

All of these things, smacking as they do of pressure groups, selfishness, determination to "have one's rights" without regard to the rights—or feelings—of others—all these things, sweeping in upon the air waves, staring coldly, blackly at us from the newspapers, are discouraging. They overshadow, like a cloud, the dream of sunny fields with quail hiding in the wind-rattled cornfields, the wood fire burning red and yellow and blue in the chimney throat, the frosty exultation of November in the waning days of the year when the sunlight is pale and thin and people go to church on Thanksgiving Day to thank God for the privilege—and the hardship—of freedom.

We will come back—oh, we will come back, because of the nostalgia that grows and grows in one's heart until it is so full that it must burst if we do not return. The cloud-shadows on the mountain sides. The stars sown at dusk in the purple valley by the city dwellers. The thin, poignant piping of a hermit thrush, deep hidden in a leafy glen. The feel of the earth beneath the leathern sole, knowing that this earth, this land, is ours, and will some day have us again. The sound of a voice, the expression in someone's eyes, the realization that what was a dream is now a dream no longer, but reality—these, these will pull us home.

It is to be feared, though, that most of America never knew much of war, except the print on a page, the vicarious and thrilling horror of a movie, and the full dinner pail. And it's up to those of you who did—and those of us who return—to prove that patriotism is not a word on the lips of a petty politician, or the shameless mouthing of a war profiteer, whether he be capitalist or laborer. No—patriotism is a harder thing than that. Somehow I think that even higher than the patriotism of the mud and the rain and the red scream of the lead searching for you, is that of the ones who in the gray mediocrity of peace can bear to see the things they worked for broken, and stoop and build them up - and of the ones who have the courage to tell people what they should be told, rather than what they want to be told.

Unless the people feel this the victory will have been in vain. And I speak not only of the learned, the wealthy, the leaders, but even more particularly of the artisan, the skilled worker, the craftsman, the builder, the man of the soil who loves the long curl of the plowed earth as the sea wanderer loves the long green swell of the sea at dawn when the color of the sky grips the heart until it almost stops beating. I speak of the clerk who knows the thrill of having customers who, when they come in, always ask for them; the policemen, the men who drive railroad engines and fill a little boy's soul with terror and ecstasy and surging joy as they pilot their flashing chargers down the ribbons of rail.

We wonder. Somehow we feel a bit stained by the Roman holiday of war's end. The dancing in the street. The drunks and the loud laughter and the people being sick in the gutter. The hurried meetings of the pressure groups. The telegrams to the congressmen. The million-dollar movies about the kids that got blown to bits for fifty bucks a month— (but in Hollywood, the battle effects are much more humanitarian).

Well—as Sandburg says,
"The woman named Tomorrow
Sits with a hairpin in her teeth
And takes her time . . ."

AFTER WORLD WAR II

Indian Summer

Already the spiced and melancholy sweetness of drying grass and leaf assails the nostrils to tell of the mortality of the year. Spring, with her girlish tears and laughter, her green rains and lemon-golden sun, is but a memory, and summer hastens to her portended doom of rendez-vous with motleyed October.

The triple stitch of the katydids sews up the dark cloth of night. The stars light their little lamps, and the moon broods, pale and melancholy, above the glens of midnight. Mists spread through the valley, and one's heart nigh bursts from its mortal cage to soar abroad on the dark wings of the night wind.

Surely this time will come again! Surely there will be buttercups and April—and dogwood blossoms spreading their pallid glory on the thin and stammering air! Surely June will walk like a young woman across the noble swelling earth and the cry of the jay will strike the noontide like a golden arrow! And surely at evening, when the dusk flows up from the valley, there will be the silver-thin fluting of the hermit thrush, piping its lonely love song among the shadowed pines!

There is so much of sadness and exultation in the heart of man. *Variabile et mutabile semper femina est*, sang the poet whose mouth has long since been stopped with clay. But it is not merely woman that is fickle. The human heart turns with the seasons, and whether we will or no, our spirit flies across the earth like an unseen bird. We are caught in the web of the past and the future, and our eyes cannot see the present for seeing other things.

And no—it will never be the same again.

Those who came back from the far corners of the earth are oppressed with that knowledge. The chief hunger of man is not physical, but spiritual. One sits bemused, staring into space, remembering the flicker of sunlight on a gull's wings, the red feet tucked up under the snowy feathers . . . forgetting the heat, the monotone of unvarying existence.

Along the Barrier Reef off the coast of Australia the Coral Sea pushes its breakers up the tawny, sun-gilt sand. The albatross glides on broad white wings, almost touching the blue combers. Far away on the rim of the horizon there is a smoke smudge that tells of another ship, hull down for destiny.

In Iloilo, in the heart of the Philippines, the ox carts move sluggishly across the square, and the natives squint at you in the bright sunlight and say, "Kumma estoca?" which means "How do you do?" The river wriggles like a serpent through the town, past the ruined Mitsui warehouses, crouching in their rubble, down to the green straits where the wind blows cool and hard all day. A sailor leans on the rail of a tramp freighter that swings at anchor in the stream, and his eyes are fretted by the red roofs of the town.

All across the world—in Hong Kong, in Germany, in France and Norway and South America, the poem is unfolded. . . . wind, sand and stars . . . the voice of the sea and the way a girl's hair ruffles in the breeze. Of such tiny things is man's heart compounded. And always and ever, there is the heart sickness, the homesickness for what has been and will never be again—for the dream that cannot be found, the door that has never been unlocked.

The true meaning of man's success is not to be had in fortunes amassed or possessions had. Rather it is in the tasting of all the fruits of all the earth—the bitter with the sweet—and the degree to which he can achieve a oneness, a unity with the lost and crying spirit of mankind.

For of such is the spirit of God.

The Middle Ages

"Miniver Cheevy, child of scorn.
Grew lean while he assailed the seasons;
He wept that he was ever born,
And he had reasons."
                                                    —E. A. Robinson

Again September comes, and by the magic alchemy of time we are suddenly translated from summer, with its brazen heat and its lush green languor, into the tragic and lovely season of fall.

As the month of harvest and the down-dipping of the year comes 'round, we are minded of the slow turn of the wheel, of the rising and the setting of stars, and of all the wild sweet sorrow that is in the heart of man. This September, more than ever before, we are conscious of the change in the shadows and of the deepened significance of the turning years for the individual.

Miniver dreamed of knights in armour. How many of us there are who, like Miniver, long for the distant romance of another time or of another country! The Middle Ages has a peculiar appeal for the romantic. I speak of the Middle Ages as comprising, perhaps, the years 1,000 to 1,600 A.D. That was the time of the great discoveries, of the explorations and the terrible and thrilling journey of Magellan, Cortez, Drake and Columbus. It was the time of jongleurs and troubadours, of knights in armour and their deeds of chivalry and individual combat, where the man of superior strength and cunning invariably won. It was the time of Francois Villon, Rostand, Kit Marlowe and Shakespeare—and all those golden-tongued bards whose spirits hallowed the Mermaid Tavern.

But, even as there was a period which we call the Middle Ages of mankind as we know it, so there is the period of the Middle Ages for each and every one of us in our own lives.

Sometime about the middle 30's one suddenly becomes aware that he has lived over half his allotted span of three score years and 10. He suddenly realizes that he has reached the top of the hill and that the descent has begun. The thought touches his heart with a cold chill, just as on these early fall mornings as fair summer droops we wake to feel the cold breath of dawn for which we sighed all summer long. A shadow is cast across one's heart—a shadow that grows as one realizes how suddenly one's body has become less apt, more clumsy. No longer can one run and play all day as in the morning of one's youth. One tires more easily, one's body tends to thicken, and one is more disposed to sit quietly and dream than to be up and doing.

"Now is the harvest of our April here—The hour as inescapable as death."

How far away the spring seems now! We remember the unpolished silver slant of rain, brightness falling from the air, and the sharp pain of April's pale greenwood, white-starred with dogwood blossoms. But it is no longer a pain—it is merely the recollection of a pain.

And there is a vast difference.

We knew than that we should sow carefully, remembering what our teachers told us. But how many of us there were who, like the grasshopper, chose merely to sing and dance! How many precious acres grew rank with weed and honeysuckle and the wild thorn because they were not sown with some more stable and productive crop!

Now we suddenly realize that this harvest which we see stretched about us is indeed our own sowing. There is much of heart-break in that realization—and yet, as we see patches of beauty scattered here and there among the topsy-turvy of our hearts' fields, we realize that the harvest is not without its recompense.

"As in a trance we view the painted wood—"

There is a supernatural quality in all aspects of nature in this time of September and the harvest and the early fall. The sun that blazed so furiously last week has suddenly become gentle and gracious. There is a reflective calm in the quality of the atmosphere—an air almost of resignation. The flowers are blue and purple and gold, dusty with sunlight—and the Indian paint brushes are as red as blood. Soon, soon, we will again walk in the spiced forests of motleyed October with the dreams of our lost April.

Already the wind is sweet with the fragrance of drying grass, the keen sweetness of ripening apples and grapes, and here and there through the dark green of the wood we see a touch of vivid orange or bright scarlet where the imminent fall has left its fragmentary print. And as we travel the winding roads that thread the mountain passes or that flow so smoothly beside the bright blue lakes or the shining and musical waters of the rivers and streams, we see the far vistas lost in a blue haze, and it is almost as though nature, like ourselves, is filled with dreams and reflections and recollections at this time of impending age and loss.

65

"The fox hounds cry among the midnight glens,
Their belling borne upon the frosty air . . ."

Yet, though youth has fled with the shadows of a vanished sun, there is still a zest for adventure that is quickened by the cool tang of this Indian summer. For as we see the hint of coming snows in the bright paint which October scatters, so, and at the same time, we see the hope of Aprils yet unborn in the faces and in the hearts of the youthful.

Whether it be in the blue of a September afternoon as we watch two young tennis players pit their strengths and skill in the white flashing geometry of the tennis match, where the red clay of the court forms a colorful background; or whether it be high in the stands of a great football stadium, tasting the cider-sweet chill of the October wind and watching the color and the torn, abrupt and stirring action of a football game; or whether it be sitting cozily by a great fireplace wherein the petaled flames, orange and yellow and blue, make color music while outside the dark and stormy wind of a cold November night beats at the walls and windows, as we listen to the bright new-minted words of an active and youthful and hope-starred mind; all of these evidence the continued zest and interest which even the Middle Ages cannot eradicate.

Rather, it sometimes seems as though the gradual cooling of the blood which one begins to notice in these middle years is more of a blessing than otherwise. The spirit is freed, as it were , from the fretting annoyance of the flesh, and can launch itself the more daringly and the more effectively into the battles which really count. For, after all, the only battles that really count are those of the spirit.

So as this time of reflection—as this post midseason of the year is interpreted in terms of our own lives, we can view the harvest with joy for what it has of good, and with little of regret for the rest.

"Farewell to summer, and a long farewell . . ."

The nights grow longer now. The orange moon that climbs the dark and brooding skies of evening casts a light more chill, more poignant. Soon the familiar constellations will appear. Orion, the Huntsman, with his belt, will stride the sky, with bright Sirius, the Dog Star, trotting after him. The long nights will be filled with memories and with dreams. As Aldous Huxley has said, the poetry of transience is like an autumnal sunset, like bells heard from a long way away, mournfully beautiful. Surely there can be no poetry of transience quite like this faery time, this Middle Age of the year!

And as the wheel turns and the year descends, we may take down a dusty book from the high shelf and, leafing through the sonnets of that sweet swan of Avon, read with deeper understanding:

"That time of year thou may'st in me behold
When yellow leaves, or none, or few, do hang
Upon these boughs which shake against the cold,
Bare ruined choirs, where late the sweet birds sang . . ."

The Green Years End

It is a wet October night. After two days of rain that has alternately misted and poured, the clouds are clearing. A half moon glows mistily through the black hieroglyphics of tree branches, and the air is stained with the taste of the rain and the nut-brown smell of the fallen leaves that lie like small water-soaked scraps of paper across the roads and the grass. October's bright blue weather is gone, and there is an ominous silence.

Tomorrow I will no longer be in my 30's.

A small boy and his father stood beside a creek in the green of springtime and watched a tiny white paper boat floating down the muddy stream.

"How slowly it goes!" cried the child.

"Yes," said the father, smiling, "but not so slowly as you think."

And I remember the battered Norlago, that old rust-pot of a refrigerator ship in which we toured the vert and gold islands of the South Pacific, and how I stood on the flying bridge with the skipper in the cool dawn of my first day aboard and watched the green smudge that was New Guinea fade in the distance.

"What speed does she make?" I asked.

"About seven or eight knots, at best," he replied, with a wry Australian grimace.

And I thought: "How slow!"

But mile after blue mile dropped astern, and the islands rose from and fell under the horizon, and even one hundred and fifty miles a day adds up to fifteen hundred miles in a ten days. And ten days can be very short.

* * *

Perhaps there is some significance in the fact that today brought the news of the death of one of our greatest lyric poets of this century. Edna St. Vincent Millay has fled the house of flesh and sought her destiny among the stars.

Remarkable indeed was that sensate and sensuous person, who, despite her love of senses, could indict the line:

"Euclid alone has looked on Beauty bare."

There is a profound lesson for us all in the tolerance of the quiet wisdom that sees, even in fields belonging to others, the eternal truths. Mathematics has never been a country of mine, yet I was compelled by that one line to gaze until I saw that indeed the plain, hard-angled truths of algebraic and geometric theorems do soar in classic stainless beauty into the stratosphere of verity.

Yet she was many sided. As she once said:

"What should I be but a prophet and a liar,
Whose mother was a leprechaun, whose father was a friar?
What should I be but the fiend's god-daughter?"

She was indeed a startlesome revelation and innovation to those upon whose gaze she burst. After her poem "Renascence" —

"All I could see from where I stood
Was three long mountains and a wood—"

which was her first success at the early age of nineteen, she went on to dip her pen in rue and scarlet and to scrawl such unforgettable poems as the following, from her sonnets:

"What lips my lips have kissed, and where, and why,
I have forgotten, and what arms have lain
Under my head till morning; but the rain
Is full of ghosts to-night, that tap and sigh
Upon the glass and listen for reply.
And in my heart there stirs a quiet pain
For unremembered lads that not again
Will turn to me at midnight with a cry.
Thus in the winter stands the lonely tree,
Nor knows what birds have vanished one by one,
Yet knows its boughs more silent than before;
I cannot say what loves have come and gone,
I only know that summer sang in me
A little while, that in me sings no more."

Things of heartbreak and beauty are, like the stars, forever beyond our finger tips. Perhaps it is because the work-a-day world cannot really understand them, and therefore cannot long remember their lessons. After the voice is stilled and the presence gone, there is only a lingering aftertone, or, as she herself put it:

"But the music of your talk
Never shall the chemistry
Of the secret earth restore.
All your lovely words are spoken.
Once the ivory box is broken,
Beats the golden bird no more."

She knew, better than most, that what we love is not really a person, but the qualities which we ascribe to a person. And she also knew that, just as when you buy a doll at a store and then paint it and dress it in clothes of your own choosing, you must never be impatient or disappointed when the doll fails to live up to the clothes in which you clad it.

There was, withal, a shining bravery in this leprechaun child as there must be in any real artist. Only a brave one could have written:

Keen

"Weep him dead and mourn as you may,
    Me, I sing as I must:
Blessed be death, that cuts in marble
    What would have sunk to dust!

Blessed be death, that took my love
    And buried him in the sea,
Where never a lie nor a bitter word
    Will out of his mouth at me!

This I have to hold to my heart,
    This to take by the hand:
Sweet we were for a summer month
    As the sun on the dry, white sand;

Mild we were for a summer month
    As the wind from over the weirs;
And blessed be death, that hushed with salt
    The harsh and slovenly years!

Who builds her a house with love for timber,
    Builds her a house of foam;
And I'd rather be bride to a lad gone down
    Than widow to one safe at home."

The harsh and slovenly years are hushed.

And the river swirls on, deep and strong and majestic, shouldering its way past the mountain's rocky ledge, past the stripped cotton fields standing mute and soggy in the late October chill, past the great plantations of sugar cane, down, down to the sonorous sea.

70

* * *

Mention of the sea brings back the sharp recollection of the long sun-splashed days of the South Pacific—the China Sea, the Philippine Sea, the hard blue choppiness of the Coral Sea, and the golden, lazy, sprawling beauty of the Great Barrier Reef where at night the Southern Cross leans down from her throne in the south to smile upon you.

H.S.M. Tomlinson, a newspaper man who in ripe middle age suddenly ran away to sea and spent the rest of his life there, tells of his first voyage in his book "the Sea and the Jungle." In it he has captured much of the feel of the world of water.

"I woke at the right moment opening my eyes with the serene and secure conviction that things are very well. The slow rocking of the ship is perfect rest. There is no sound but the faint tap-tap of something loose on the deck and responding to the ship's movement. The cabin is strangely illuminated to its deepest corner by an extraordinary light, as though the intense glow of a rare dawn had penetrated even our iron-work. On the white top of the cabin a bright moon quivers about, the shine from live waters sent up through the round of our port, when we lean over. The port shows first the roof of the alleyway dappled with bright reflection; then a circle of sky, which the horizon soon halves; and then the dazzling white and blue of the near waves; we reverse."

You can almost smell the cleanness of the salt-washed air!

* * *

"Ne cherchez plus mon coeur; les bêtes l'ont mangé."

Tomorrow is a new decade. How little time there is, and how much to be done! And in this season of October's death when the color of the wood cries out upon the stammering air and the flavor of frost is in the wind, there is, more than ever, the knowledge of our finite nature.

Truly, as the prophet has said, Man is as grass; the wind passeth over it and it is no more.

Yeats has compressed and distilled the essence of this time in one of his poems where he says:
"The woods were round them and the yellow leaves
Fell like faint meteors in the gloom and once
A rabbit old and lame limped down the path.
Autumn was over him."

Yes, autumn comes over us all—and it is always sooner than we think. Time is the one stream– the damming of which we know not of.

Yet, as the year turns, and as the fall brings back Orion and the

71

Pleiades, we are warmed by the very flaming knowledge of the inevitability of time.

For if winter comes, there must be spring in the offing.

And how delicious it is to always contemplate the coming of one more spring!

The Face of the Earth

A book entitled *The Face of the Earth* has just been published. It is by H.M. Tomlinson, one of the most magnetic figures of literature—largely because of one daring step that he took.

Nearly half a century ago he was a reporter on a London newspaper. Not altogether happy about what he was doing, he had thought much about changing his life, but like so many of us, had done nothing about it.

One day he was talking with a friend who was the captain of a tramp steamer. This steamer was about to depart for the South Atlantic, where it was to journey some 2,000 miles up a South American river into the steaming green jungle on what was the first such voyage ever attempted. The captain tried to talk Tomlinson into going along on the trip. The two men were standing on a street corner in the rain waiting for a bus which was already visible down the street. Tomlinson told his friend that if as many as three people got on the bus before it reached them, he would go on the voyage. At the last bus stop before it reached them, two passengers got on—which seemed to doom the possibility of his going—but the captain ran down the street to meet the bus and got on before it reached Tomlinson, thereby averting what would have been a major disaster.

Tomlinson went, and, wrote his beautiful and haunting book, "The Sea and the Jungle," and a magnificent literary career was launched.

Daring is an essential element of greatness.

The face of the earth at this present time is not such as to be reassuring to the potential traveler. Indeed, there is grave danger that we will be so comforted by the tranquility and the peace here at home that we will refuse to lift up our eyes and look abroad.

After all, there is much to enthrall us in this autumn season. Freed from the blazing heat of the summer, we greet with pleasure the faint chill of the air. The World Series is still ahead—relic of a lost time. More in season is the sound of boys kicking a football, the smell of burning leaves, the spurting deliciousness of juicy apples, or the tart, smoky taste of muscadines.

We wake in the night and lie there in the frosty darkness hearing a dog bark and the distant throbbing of a plane that shoves through the moonsilvered heavens, and we are snatched away into the long ago.

We remember what it was like to go back to school—the oily reek of the floor, the dusty smell of the chalk. We remember how once in the third grade we climbed into a tall pine tree to eat our lunch and, while topping it off with an apple, accidentally and unexpectedly removed one of our baby teeth—so unexpectedly, indeed, that we almost fell out of the tree from shock.

There is a strange and mystical union of past and present in this harvest time. Now as never before we appreciate Housman's poems, his familiar

"With rue my heart is laden
             For golden friends I had,
For many a rose-lipped maiden
             And many a lightfoot lad."

So many golden ones have gone in the past year—blown away into the beyond like autumn leaves!

Not long ago we went up onto the Cumberland Plateau to spend a week at the state park. By the time we arrived, it was practically vacant. Beside the bright blue lake the trees still stood in summer green, but here and there the scarlet of a leaf showed, and the tawny sun shone with a lessening fever. Already the autumn spell was come, the sky was smoky blue, and the harsh cry of the jays sounded tired and dispirited. At night a huge white moon moved sedately among the dark tangled tree branches, and we could hear the faint and far away honking of geese driving their wedged way southward through the wine-dark air.

One morning we drove along Pigeon Ridge into Crossville near by, and, part of the autumn, there were the old men sitting on the courthouse lawn in the paling sunlight, chewing tobacco, and whittling on sticks of aromatic cedar with ancient hands that looked like pieces of driftwood.

In autumn all the smells of the earth become quickened and sharpened. The rich, cold smell of leaf mold, the spicy fragrance of dry grass, and the clean, nut-brown smell of the woods all stir our hearts to the realization that the hunger of the spirit is the hugest hunger of all.

It is a time to especially enjoy one's friends. Friendship is like old wine in its tartness, its sweetness, and its headiness. Sometimes it has to be kept for a long time to be properly aged. Yet occasionally by some strange chemistry, it is old when first we find it.

To come close to another being is one of the rare and intoxicating moments of a lifetime. We delude ourselves into a sense of security, of belonging, or possessing—but actually we are the loneliest creatures in the universe. Alone we came into the world, and alone we must leave it. But the snatching of a few bright splinters of time when we belong to one another (or feel that we do) is one of the most precious delights. Then we know with certainty the eloquence in stillness—the crinkling of the eyes, the warmth of a handshake, the vibrance of a silence whose meaning transcends words.

Yet on the face of the earth there are things that we must see, that we must realize.

Recently we received a letter from Oliver Hodge, formerly professor of modern language at the University of Chattanooga and now somewhere in Red-shadowed Europe, "where," he says, I feel so keenly what it is to be without the dream we have had in America." He goes on to say, "I see hundreds of people every day who look as if they hardly cared whether they lived or died. The whole scrimy deal has worked itself out here. Our so lightly accepted feeling that every man deserves his chance—that the individual is sacred—that's a bitter joke here. Our offices—Engineers—are in a former workers' lager. We have many DP's working for us. I personally deal with dozens of these people every week. I can't tell you what a living warning these people are—a warning of what cruelty, exploitation, greed can do to human beings. The victims are dehumanized—have lost all sense of their value as human beings."

He then goes on to discuss the recent issue of *Time* in which a Cleveland Press editorial was quoted:

"Something happened to us as a people—something serious.

"We have gained much in that last half-century.

"We have lost something, also . . .

"Has what we gained been more important than what we lost?"

And he ends: "The whole world is ripe for a revelation of some kind. We are really in one of those dismal bogdowns of history where we can go only up."

While we are enjoying to the fullest the haunting beauty of this magic time, we must draw inspiration from it for concrete action, that we may better the face of the earth.

Now is the golden season, the time of remembering. But, as someone has so well said—happy memories must be planned for in advance.

What will our memories be in autumn 10 years hence?

Now is the time to decide.

Thanks and Courage

November has come and gone—and with it another Thanksgiving Day.

This Thanksgiving was a day of gorgeous November weather. The sky was sun-drenched, pale blue, and a thin wind rustled the dead leaves on the ground. Some of the oaks still wore their brick-red foliage, and here and there among the whispering leafy carpet underfoot, one spied a bright leaf, orange or scarlet or lemon-colored. At noon there was the steamy deliciousness of roast turkey with dressing and gravy and cranberry sauce, the fragrance and taste of piping hot rolls, butter-soaked; the spicy goodness of sweet potatoes, and rich, cold, creamy milk—Thanksgiving dinner with all the trimmings. Then, that afternoon, there was the football game. The game was like the day in that it sparkled. It was close and thrilling, full of violence and surprise. And the blanket of pale gold sunlight that spread across the stadium and the trampled turf of the field was just enough to keep out the frosty chill of the air.

But somehow this Thanksgiving seemed a bit different.

Perhaps it was just that our thinking was accented by the community church service that we attended that morning atop Lookout Mountain.

This year the community service was held in the new Baptist church, with the pastor, Dale Larew, as host. George Murphy, rector of the Church of the Good Shepherd, led in the Thanksgiving litany and prayer, and Sam Wiley, of the Presbyterian Church, delivered the sermon.

The church itself is one of inspiration and beauty. Built of neat red brick, it has a lofty roof and a white steeple that points its delicate, slender spire heavenward into the clear mountain air. The interior of the church is white painted, light and spacious, and was full of the gay colors of the crowd that thronged into it. Through the tall windows the blue sky smiled, and the late November sunlight poured in. The chrysanthemums massed behind the chancel were golden and bronze and copper colored, and in the singing together of the old Thanksgiving hymns—"Come, Ye Thankful People, Come," and "America, the Beautiful"—there was a warmth of enthusiasm and oneness and worship that had much the same glow as the melted-butter sunlight.

76

Sam Wiley took as a text that portion of the 28th chapter of Acts which tells how Paul, on his journey to Rome, met certain of his friends and disciples at a small town outside Rome, "whom, when Paul saw, he thanked God, and took courage."

The subject of the address was "Thanks and Courage."

It was pointed out that we have so many things for which to be thankful. One of the loveliest of his quotations was the following, which we understand was written by someone named Hazel Parker:

"The harvest has been taken.

The hearts of men in other lands may be slow to give thanks this year. But here, where streets still are quiet and there is more of laughter than of crying, the heart has reason to feel gladness for many things.

For these desperate days of proof that man does not live by food and sleep alone, a truth that our fathers knew, and we know now, past ever forgetting it.

For the bigness of people who never forget that there are some enemies, too, sick for the quietness of remembered Sundays, for white tablecloths and the sound of footsteps strolling by.

For the snow that falls softly over the statue of Lincoln in the library yard, resting like a blessing upon his big feet; and for the sun that comes finally to brush the snow from his sunken cheeks.

For long rows of books, musty and new, in libraries everywhere; and for some words of Jefferson's that may be found there.

For the sincere idealism of men like Richard Llewellyn, who says: "There is no room for pride in any man. There is no room for unkindness. All men are born the same, and equal."

For the open doors of churches, for the faith of men and women who sit inside with bared heads.

For the comfort to be found in daily things—in an uncensored newspaper, a bowl of hot soup, a steaming bath.

For the deep, rich smell of soil upturned, and for rough hands everywhere that know the feel of the earth.

For shuttered windows in little towns, shading the peace that old folks find in twilight.

For friendship and laughter shared; and for pain that passes, leaving the mind clean-washed.

For compassion that will save the earth some day, when men and women can no longer support the knowledge that there are children who lie down at night and dream of bread.

For houses lived in and loved, for the silent ties between brother and brother, and for the love of mothers for small sons with dirty faces.

For work to be done, and strength to do it. For youth, above all, that insists upon life on its own clear terms, knowing that death may be the penalty of insistence."

The heart of the matter, though—the kernel of the whole talk—was the emphasis laid on the conclusion that we, like Paul, having thanked God, may take courage.

We may take courage in the fact that we are not alone.

Those people who ally themselves with God are never alone. They can rely on a strength that is greater than themselves.

This was the strength of the Hebrew nation, God's chosen people.

This, too, was the strength of the little struggling band of refugees who braved the iron-gray anger of the icy North Atlantic and the rigors of the wilderness that was America in order to establish this nation and to establish the first Thanksgiving Day.

But as we left the church and went out again into the blue and brown and gold of the November day, we were troubled—troubled about whether as a nation we are that spiritual strength which once we were. Are there, perhaps, too many in this country to whom Thanksgiving Day was just another holiday—another football game—rather than a day on which to thank God and take courage?

Watching the brown leaves as they spiraled earthward, and feeling the approach of winter and its long nights, we were conscious of a slight chill in the air—or was it in our heart?

Memorial Day

Memorial Day—any Memorial Day-is time to remember.

We forget so quickly.

Perhaps it is well to forget some things, but there are other things we should not forget.

Christina Rosetti wrote:

"When I am dead, my dearest,

Sing no sad songs for me;

Plant thou no roses at my head,

Nor shady cypress tree;

Be the green grass above me

With showers and dewdrop wet;

And if thou wilt, remember,

And if thou wilt, forget."

In our day-to-day living, the accent seems to be more on the forgetting than on the remembering.

Robert Nathan has a poem about it. He calls it "Torpedo 8." It is about a torpedo bomber squadron, and it ends:

"They were good boys. They didn't have much to remember,

Just a few years, and the high school dances, and the mistletoe over the door

And the honeysuckle in June, and the frost in November.

They didn't have much time.

They didn't have long to be young. They saved America for us.

Nobody thinks about them any more."

But Memorial Day is time to remember—time to remember the disappointment that the war dead must feel for the bungling way we have handled the victories purchased with their lives.

Out of World War I came a poem by Grantland Rice that bespeaks how their dreams live on:

"Where rain-wet crosses know the dawn that gleams,

Safe from the crashing shell, the raw steel's thrust,

They face the resurrection of their dreams

Where only songs now live above their dust."

As we see these southern mountains of ours garbed in the beauty of early summer, our hearts are pierced by the beauty of the earth the fallen left behind them.

A week or so ago we drove south along the top of Lookout Mountain to Cleveland. The day was one of sun and showers, the purple rhododendron and pink-white laurel were in full bloom, and as we passed along the eastern brow of the mountain above MacLemore's Cove, we thought again how that cove would appeal to the spirits of the boys from this area.

At that point an arm or offshoot of Lookout Mountain forks off to the northeast. That branch of the mountain is known as Pigeon Mountain. Between Pigeon Mountain and the main body of Lookout lies MacLemore's Cove, a quiet, fertile valley of winsome green beauty that surpasses anything that words can tell. What a lovely scene for the tired spirit of a boy to come home to!

And we remembered again T.P. Cameron Wilson's little poem about the English boys who died in battle, "Sportsmen in Paradise:"

"They left the fury of the fight,
        And they were very tired.
The gates of Heaven were open, quite
        Unguarded and unwired.
There was no sound of any gun,
        The land was still and green;
Wide hills lay silent in the sun,
        Blue valleys slept between.

They saw, far off, a little wood
        Stand up against the sky,
Knee-deep in grass a great tree stood . . .
        Some lazy cows went by . . .
There were some rooks sailed overhead,
        And once a church bell pealed.
'God! but it's England,' someone said,
        'And there's a cricket-field!'"

Perhaps because this Memorial Day on June 3 is peculiarly of and for the South, we think especially of the War Between the States and the heroes of that time.

The flood of battle in and about Chattanooga—bloody Chickamauga, the fog-shrouded Battle Above the Clouds, and the Battle of Missionary Ridge—are now no more than the remembered music of a dream or of a symphony heard long ago.

But we must never forget the bright spirits of those who gave their lives—those brave with the crimson courage of young Sam Davis, who chose to be hanged rather than betray a friend.

Adelaide Rowell has written beautifully of Sam's gallant death in her book, "On Jordan's Stormy Banks," and at the end she tells how a mountain preacher called Hallooya, who was Sam's friend, risked capture and death to be with Sam at the end:

"Steady and unhurried, he [Sam] walked up the steps of the scaffold. Captain Armstrong was at his side. At the top, Chaplain Young and Vanpelt waited for him.

"'Mr. Young,' he said, 'will you sing On Jordan's Stormy Banks I Stand'?'

"He looked afar toward the smoke-blue mountains . . . back again to the scene about him . . . and last of all to the mountain man who had come to be with him.

"A hush had come over the body of armed men. Though the sun shone, it seems as though a great wave of cold air had enveloped the valley.

"Hallooya stepped forward and no one stopped him. His voice rang out as though he challenged Hell to deny what he was saying.

"'The Lord air my shepherd. I'll not be wantin' fer ary thing. He takens me down to walk with Him in the green fields along o' the leetle crick a-runnin' thar. . . .'

"His eyes were on Sam as long as the boy could see him. Then he lifted his face up to heaven, the tears washing down his rugged cheeks. His voice rose in a triumphant shout:

"'Yea, though you send me down into the valley of the shadder of Death hitself, I'll not be afeered. Lord Jesus, I know you'll be a-walkin' along of me, holdin' my hand, comfortin. . .'"

"He could say no more.

"Sam had crossed over the turbulent river and had come into the green, sunny fields on the other side."

Memory is a golden book

And there are no more shining pages than those to which we turn on Memorial Day—the time to remember.

Appreciation of Heroism

August and the end of summer speak to us of the turn of the year, and there is a certain sadness implicit in this season.

A few days ago an event occurred that served to deepen that sadness. Jeffrey Farnol died.

John Jeffrey Farnol was born in England in the year 1878. He began to write at the age of nineteen. From 1902 to 1910 he lived in the City of New York. While there he wrote short stories and painted scenery for the Astor Theater. Since 1910 he has been back in England.

He was a novelist.

Jeffrey Farnol wrote novels about one of the most romantic periods in English history. The setting of his books was usually in England during the eighteen hundreds. One of his favorite and recurrent themes was that of the son and heir of an aristocratic family, who tired of the fobbishness and artificiality of his own social stratum, had become interested in pugilism. The young man was invariably a magnificent physical specimen and a ferocious fighter, and after a series of spine-tingling adventures, he married the sensuous creature who was the heroine.

But it is much more fitting that Mr. Farnol's writing speak for itself.

In "Beltane, The Smith," we find the following description of early morning in an English woodland:

"The morning was yet young when Beltane fared forth into the world, a joyous, golden morning thrilling with the glad song of birds and rich with a thousand dewy scents; a fair, sweet, joyous world it was indeed whose glories, stealing in at eye and ear, filled him with their gladness.

Again, in "The Loring Mystery," we have the following description of dawn in the city:

"Slowly the great city began to awake; from a myriad chimneys smoke curled lazily against the brightening sky; doors opened; the erstwhile empty streets began to echo with the tramp of feet, the tramp of horses and the grind of wheels . . . upon graveled thoroughfares. There was a ring of hoofs, the shout and cry of the drivers that was the mighty voice of London town."

One of the familiar marks of any of Farnol's books is the element of storm and conflict. For example, again from "The Loring Mystery":

"Roused by this growing uproar, David glanced round about him from wild-tossing trees and swaying thickets to a gloomy heaven where crept a vast black cloud, an inky pall which, as he gazed, was riven asunder by a jagged lightning-flash followed by a crashing thunderclap that seemed to stun the very wind to silence. And in this quiet came the rain, a few great drops to splash upon David's upturned brow—very grateful and cooling. Then up rose the wind again, a bellowing fury now, to tear at groaning trees until they bowed and cracked, to fill the swirling darkness with flying twigs and leaves."

His descriptions of the evening and the night are wonderful. In "The High Adventure" we find the following:

"On strode he through a fragrant dusk wherein stars paled to the evergrowing splendour of the rising, full-orbed moon.

"Gradually the narrow lane dwindled to a winding track that led him upwards until, reaching the top of this ascent, he might look down over a wide prospect-field, hedgerow and sombre woods, to the looming swell of the Downs, vague and mysterious, beyond which lay the sea."

And the battles and fights are without parallel. For example, again from "The High Adventure":

"And now in the gloomy arch beside the gate was a battle fierce and fell and always grimly silent, except for the shock of blows, the hoarse gasping of breath, the quick, ceaseless shuffle of feet. Broad back to the wall, Jeremy fought, blow for blow. Men fell and rose again, leapt to smite and be smitten, groaned and cursed, swore at and encouraged one another, for, sheltered now in the angle of wall and door, Jeremy fought as one born to it, swift of foot and eye, of parry and counterstroke, judging speed and distance with the passionless calm of the true fighting man."

The damsels whom Farnol chose as his heroines were all of a sort. As an example, we have selected a brief description from "Beltane, the Smith":

"Eyes long, thick-lashed and darkly blue that looked up a while into his and anon were hid 'neath languorous-drooping lids; a nose tenderly aquiline; lips, red and full, that parted but to meet again in sweet and luscious curves; a chin white, and round and dimpled.

"This Beltane saw 'twixt hood and wimple, by aid of the torch that flickered against the wall; and she conscious of his look, stood with white hands demurely crossed upon her rounded bosom, with eyes abased and scarlet lips apart, as one who waits—expectant."

Even the descriptions of minutiae are such as to warm the heart. There is a glad freshness of color, a clean fragrance about his writing that blows like a fresh wind and sweeps away the noxious vapors that pervade so much of modern writing. In "The Quest of Youth" we find the following:

"After some while, his hunger gloriously appeased, he leaned back to survey this pleasant room, massive rafters above, red tiles below and a great, open fireplace where logs crackled cheerily, beside which stood a pair of riding boots, newly polished, their toes and heels sedately together."

There is a story, and a good story, in each and every one of Jeffrey Farnol's books. The heroes of the books are heroic and the heroines are worthy of worship.

In this day and age, that is truly a rarity.

One of the consolations of art is its immortality. Though "dying summer brings her fruits to ground," the fruits of the artist live on and on.

And youthful hearts, now and hereafter, will long cherish Jeffrey Farnol's golden apples of romance.

Charlie and the Mule

It's strange, the things that stick in your memory and don't fade. I remember when I was a little boy: The bees in the persimmon trees, and the blue, wooly heat of summer, and the pipe that came out through the side of our house and drained the refrigerator. The drip from the pipe made a cool, damp place beside the wall of the house where mint grew, and I would crush mint in my hand and the sharp, sweet smell would stab me. I remember the ice wagon with its great black mules, and Bill Pugh, the iceman, almost as big and black as the mules—and the way he would bellow, "I—i-ce-man-n!" and then come toiling up the hill, sweating and bowed low under the 100-pound block of ice. . . . And I remember Charlie and the mule.

It must have been right after World War I that Charlie Degrado came to the mountain. He came to work for Mrs. Engle, who lived up near the top of the Incline. Charlie was an Italian, which in itself was enough to make him notorious if not famous. Mrs. Engle put him to work back on her farm back where the Fairyland Golf Course is now. Ernie Penley lived close by, and Mr. Kington and the Bettises and the Stewarts. Mr. Kington had a mare named Julie that was lovely to look at, and we later owned her, and a gelding named Buster that broke my heart—but that's another story. Anyhow, Charlie got a mule and went to work. Shortly thereafter Mrs. Engle moved back on the farm. She has since died, but Charlie and his mule have lived on and worked on, and still do.

It's not the same mule, of course. That's been over 30 years ago, and mules just don't last that long. But Charlie has.

It's always been the same. His buggy is filled with boxes and crates of berries and fruits and vegetables and all sorts of good things. It comes ambling along behind the ambling mule. Then it stops and Charlie asks in his broken English if you want to buy anything. Usually you do. His produce is always delicious and there's—well, there's just something about doing business with Charlie that does you good.

If you drive along the road that skirts the south boundary of the golf course, the curving, hilly land from which you can see the valley and the mountain stretching away to the south, you are likely to see Charlie out working in his garden. Sometimes the mule is working, too. Some-

85

times the mule is just grazing, or just being a mule. But Charlie is always working.

The other day a friend of mine was telling about some people he had succeeded in getting out of Germany as DP's. He had guaranteed to look after them, and had sent them money to come over, and had put them on a farm he owned. They didn't like the farm. He moved them to town, and the young man of the family got a job. They are not quite making their own way yet, but the other day they announced they were going to buy an automobile. My friend objected. They aren't yet self-sustaining, and he's still guarantor for them. They insisted. "All right," he said. "When you do you're also getting a ticket back to Germany." One wonders whether they are willing to sell their good life in a land of opportunity for an automobile. One would never wonder that about Charlie. His sense of values is a lot better than that of most of his customers, were the truth but known.

Once when I was 11 or 12 there was forest fire below the bluffs at our farm. Our farm lay between the Engle place and the brow of the mountain. After supper one night, Dad and I rode to the bluff and watched the flaming holocaust below. The red glare filled the sky and there was a roaring sound as the wind fanned the lashing flames to hotter fury. Whenever the sparks started fire up on top where we were, we beat it out with pine boughs. Finally it began to die down and we headed home, and a soft rain began before I even got to sleep, and that ended it. You could always depend on Charlie to help.

Raspberries, strawberries, gooseberries, blackberries, cherries, grapes, cantaloupes, watermelons, tender sweet Golden Bantam corn, lima beans, green beans—oh, every sort of good thing can be gotten from Charlie and his mule. And always he raises tiny yellow tomatoes that he gives to all the children along the way.

But the best thing you get from him is intangible and priceless. It's his love of the earth of this adopted land of his; his quick willing, work-hardened hands; his gentleness and goodness and the love that seems to glow in his seamed and weather-beaten face.

The other day I was driving home up the Ochs Highway. It was high noon, and a savage sun beat down on the June-green mountain and the hot, sticky tar highway where the tourists troop soddenly along in their quest for the ultimate. As we rounded a curve, there ahead of us was a mule, picking its newly shod way daintily up the road.

"There's Charlie and his mule," I said.

Sure enough, at the forward end of the mule, there was Charlie. He always walks to and from town leading the mule, when he takes it to the blacksmith. The road is too slick to risk hurting the mule, which might fall if he rode.

As we passed, my daughter called out to him and waved.

And the way his face lit up and the sunshine of his voice, and the glad quick wave of his hand carried more freight than a dozen automobiles could ever manage.

Somehow we can't escape the feeling that one of the best parts of our lives is represented by Charlie and his mule!

Note Written on a Rainy Night

There was the heat, the towering heat that wrapped you in thick wool, and then the rain came. It poured in torrents until the streets were rivers of swirling water, and then it stopped, and the heat was there again.

It was like Manila when you felt the sweat trickle down inside your shirt and then it rained and then there was the sweat again, until you could not tell which was rain and which was sweat.

But tonight was cool, and in the cold darkness you heard the sibilant whisper of the rain on the roof and the gurgling of the downspouts. And you lay on cool white sheets and read "The Bridges at Toko Ri" in the July 6 issue of *Life*.

The story of Harry Brubaker, jet pilot on the Savo, is a tiny perfect microcosm. The freezing gray water off Korea; the fear and the bravery of men who fight for a nation that has virtually forgotten them; those swift falcons, the Banshees, that scourge the convoluted and misshapen mountains of North Korea: these are the background. In the foreground are Harry, the young lawyer from Denver, a veteran of World War II who hates the war but fights because "the world has always depended on voluntary men"; Beer Barrel, the giant Texan naval officer, who stands on the end of the flight deck, and, with his paddles, waves the planes onto or away from the bucking carrier; Mike Forney, who wears a green opera hat and pilots the helicopter that fishes the men out of the icy sea; Adm. George Tarrant, called "George the Tyrant," who lost his own two sons in World War II, and who has a deep affection for Brubaker; Nancy, Harry's wife, who comes to Yokosuka with their two little girls, and last and most important, the bridges at Toko Ri.

Brubaker and the admiral were talking: Finally, Brubaker asked: 'Do we have to knock out those particular bridges?'

"'Yes we must. I believe without question that some morning a bunch of Communist generals and commissars will be holding a meeting to discuss the future of the war. And a messenger will run in with the news that the Americans have knocked out even the bridges at Toko-Ri. And that little thing will convince the Russians that we will never stop . . . never give in . . . never weaken in our purpose . . .'"

There is some of the same feeling in "Tales of the South Pacific," but they were mostly yarns such as your hear in bull sessions in the drawing room when you are waiting to go on watch. "The Cruel Sea" had a touch of it. "The Caine Mutiny" had more, but it was longer and the explosive effect was softened by being spread, but in this story of the Bridges at Toko-Ri, there is nothing to diffuse it, and it has a powerful, jolting lesson.

Toward the end, much of the story is wrapped up in one brief paragraph:

"Now the sky was empty and the helicopter stood burned out in the rice field, and in the ditch there was no one beside him. Harry Brubakei, a 29-year-old lawyer from Denver, Colorado was alone in a spot he had never intended to defend in a way he had not understood. In his home town at that moment the University of Colorado was playing Denver in their traditional basketball game. The stands were crowded with more than 8,000 people, and not one of them gave a damn about Korea . . ."

And when the story is done, you hear again the falling rain and you look at the white sheets and the mellow light of the reading lamp over your bed and you think of the men that are away on the other side of the world, wallowing in the mud and filth and hearing the metallic sound of the guns that scream and tear at them. And you hate the shallow easy artificiality of your own life—the parties, the swimming pools, the softness and the decadence of it all. You even remember a poem you wrote back in 1943—one that went:

"In June, my good friend said,
our daughter will return.
        I thought: The air is very chill
        no doubt the air-conditioner is maladjusted.
Then we will go (he thus went on)
into the higher mountains for a change
—a change of air. They say, you know,
that everyone who hitherto has gone
to Europe or the shore—
        (and here he paused
        to chew a pink shrimp)
now will go
into the mountains,
Which is practical.
        A bit of an inconvenience, don't you think?
        I asked: The crowding and the—you know what I mean?
Yes. But they say, I hear,

that on the shore the beach is very poor,
all scummy with the oil from tankers sunk.
        And skulls of men upon the ocean's floor,
        I thought. And pitiful burned flesh of
        sailors, too, no doubt.

———

        I felt the cold dry wind
        upon my spine
        and heard the crystal
        tinkling of ice.
You are quite right. I heartily rejoined
—this is the war—the hour of sacrifice."

In this age of the prefabricated, the predigested and the tritely pack-
aged, it is gratifying to know that there is a man who can still carve a
jewel of a story in fine, precise and glowing words—a jewel that has all
the cutting qualities and the iridescent beauty of a diamond.

Thank you Mr. Michener!

Forests of the Night

Winter is like an etching, all black and white and gray. The stark ugliness and evil of the world contrasts sharply with the white of the snow and the clean deep beauty of wind combed sky. It is the time for thinking more than for doing.

And, speaking of thinking, the news stories out of Mississippi about the Negro sharpshooter who went berserk and shot several people bring to mind one of the most unforgettable episodes in the writings of the late Thomas Wolfe.

It is in the eighth chapter of his book, "The Web and the Rock," the chapter that is titled "The Child by Tiger." Briefly stated, it is the story of a Negro man named Dick Prosser, who worked for a family in what we presume to be Asheville, Wolfe's home town.

He was a wonderful marksman with a rifle and the boys used to delight in seeing him shoot. Furthermore, he knew how to box and knew a great deal about footfall.

All in all, he was one of the most attractive and delightful personalities one would care to see.

But after being jilted by a girl who also worked for his employers, he seemed to go completely off his rocker.

It was on a Saturday night.

That same afternoon the protagonist of Wolfe's story and his friend had been fooling around the basement room where Dick lived when they saw an automatic army rifle there.

And to go on in Wolfe's words:

"This was 4 o'clock on Saturday afternoon. Already, there was a sombre moaning of the wind, gray storm clouds sweeping over, the threat of snow was in the air.

"The snow fell that night. It began at 6 o'clock. It came howling down across the hills. It swept in on them from the Southwest. By 7 o'clock the air was blind with sweeping snow, the earth was carpeted, the streets were numb. The storm howled on, around houses warm with crackling fires and shaded light. All life seemed to have withdrawn into thrilling isolation. A horse went by up in the street with muffled hoofs. . . . A little after 2 o'clock next morning, he (George Webber, the boy about whom the book is written) was awakened by the ringing of a bell. It was a hard fast stroke that he had never heard before. Bronze with peril, clangorous through the snow-numbed silence of the air, it had a quality of instancy and menace he had never known before. He leaped up and ran to the window to look for the telltale glow against the sky. But it was no fire. Almost before he looked,those deadly strokes beat in upon his brain the message that this was no alarm for fire. It was a savage, brazen tongue calling the town to action, calling mankind against the menace of some peril—secret, dark, unknown, greater than fire or flood could ever be."

What had happened was that Dick Prosser had been drinking, and had gotten into an argument with his girlfriend's husband. Shortly before midnight, crazed by jealousy and drink, he went and got his rifle and returned to kill the husband, shooting him squarely through the back of the head. Two policemen came to investigate. Dick had killed one of them, then killed the other. He started uptown, walking up the middle of the snowy street, shooting everyone that came in sight. He killed an old Negro man and he shot another white man, permanently crippling him. Then he killed another policeman.

"Then Dick rose, pivoted like a soldier in his tracks, and started back down the street, right down the center of the car tracks, straight as a string, right out of town."

The snow was deep, and the crowd that formed in answer to the brazen clangor of the bell had no difficulty following him. They had dogs, and the men and the dogs trailed him across a field into a little wood.

They surrounded him there and he killed two or three more men before he ran out of ammunition. Then he ran stumblingly down a few yards to a creek, sat down on a rock, unlaced his shoes, took them off, placed them neatly at his side and stood up like a soldier, erect, in his bare feet, and faced the mob.

They closed in on him and killed him.

Wolfe quotes Blake's immortal

"Tiger! Tiger! burning bright
In the forests of the night,
What immortal hand or eye
Could shape thy fearful symmetry?"

And in conclusion, he uses the following language which seems so aptly to describe the dark mystery of man's sometime behavior:

"He came from darkness. He came out of the heart of the secret and undiscovered South. He came by night, just as he passed by night. He was . . . a friend, a brother, and a mortal enemy, an unknown demon . . . a tiger and a child."

Memorial—The Day After

"I remember, I remember—"
—Thomas Hood

Ten years have passed since our personal war—the middle war of present generations usually referred to as World War II.

It seems impossible. The thickening of the girth, the greying and balding, the stealthy advance of stodginess and resignation—all these attest the passing of a decade. But still the heart rebels against what the mind knows, and we fly back, back on the wings of memory.

The pictures flash upon the screen of the mind like color slides, but they have three dimensions, and also the sound, the smell and the feel.

The sea:

"The sea was calm, glassy. The last stars were paling in the brightening air. On the rim of the world the trembling colors of imminent dawn burned cool and fragile. The ships about us were like toys carved of ebony and set upon a green glasstopped table. They seemed scarcely to move. I sat on a gray painted step of a gun-tub, drinking the chill, sweet air, and watching the night sink into the sea like thin purple mist that floated down, gentle and sad out of the sky. Soon day would break. The tropic sun would leap from the blue green water with a thunder of cascading molten gold, and the clangor of the heat would begin."

The jungle:

"The jeep ran smoothly along the wide packed-coral road. Coral makes a road much like chert. On either hand the jungle loomed up, thick, dark and brooding. Huge trees towered upward of a hundred feet into the damp gray air. Great vines, like giant pythons, coiled tightly, smotheringly, around the tree trunks. Bats, having a wing span of over a yard, flapped through the green shadows, and along the road flew tiny dark-blue birds, that flittered like swifts, or even more, like butterflies, in an aimless, jagged fashion. Palm trees towered smoothly up, with clusters of coconuts hanging high up in the lower fringe of their pale green foliage."

The islands:

"It was an island of incredible color. The city of Iloilo was mostly a

93

rubble—an inanimate sermon of man's greatest illusion, which is the illusion of permanency. We anchored in the straits near the mouth of the river. The water in the straits was dark blue, swept by the wind that blew hard all day and all night, and all about us were the multi-colored sails of the outrigger canoes. We went ashore and walked up the street that wound alongside the river where stood the bombed-out Mitsui warehouses. On the square in the center of town we witnessed a colorful parade of American and Filipino soldiers. Later we met a Spanish family who were connected with Elizalde and Company of Manila, and at night we sat in the patio of their home in the darkness under the blazing stars and sipped brandy and talked of war and peace. A few days later we rode out into the mountains where they were still fighting, and down along the coast where the gape-jawed LST's were loading for the invasion of Negros Island. There were ancient stone churches with green bronze bells, and water buffalo that slowly lumbered along the road, drawing great wooden-wheeled carts. And there was the bright scarlet of the flame tree which is called in Spanish and in Togalog "arbol de fuego."

Australia:

"The first morning when we awoke in Sydney harbor we saw the bright colored tile roofs of the city and the Van Gogh color of the water and the sky and high above the harbor, the arching web of the bridge. Units of the British fleet steamed into harbor that golden morning, weary and battered from the fighting up toward Japan. The sailors were drawn up as for parade on the broad flight decks of the carriers, and the bands were playing. The ships had iron names like the Black Prince and the Invincible. And in the streets of the city when dusk fell and the light flared up, the cold air came down from the Blue Mountains to the west and the news boys cried their wares with the same haunting, stridently musical note that is the same all over the world."

War is but the projection of the individual's struggle with the world about him. Its most horrid danger is its peculiar fascination—a fascination that springs from man's instinct to lose himself utterly in the doing of something. All of us become so tired, so achingly tired of being what Cabell has aptly termed "the lackey of prudence and half-measures."

Quite by accident the other day on the elevator we heard a young man say that he had been in New Guinea with that fabulous 32nd Infantry Division, which suffered over 300 per cent casualties. He was in the terrible march from Port Moresby on the west coast of New Guinea across the Owen Stanley Mountains, (whose snow-capped peaks thrust up to 13,000 or 14,000 feet into the shocking blue of the tropic sky), to Buna and the bloody battle there. He said that more than the battles he remembered the awful march through the mountains and the men who became sick and could not go on and had to be left to die. (We remembered the road that soared up from the jungle at Oro Bay, the bushy-headed natives spearing fish along the shore, and the baleful green eye of the jungle waiting a chance to move in again.) And there flooded in upon us, as the sea floods in through a torpedo-shattered bulkhead, the thought of all the casualties of war—those who lost their lives; those less fortunate, who merely lost part of their bodies, and lastly and most tragic, those who lost part of their minds or part of their souls.

What of those who came back, only to be sniped off by alcoholism? What of those whose nerves had been strung so taut that they snapped? What about the Indian boy who helped to raise the flag at Okinawa? And what about Sgt. John Doe (or Gunners Mate 3.C. Roe) who sits in a psychiatric ward in a veteran's hospital and looks at a blank gray wall and sees nothing? (Or is it nothing?)

Let's remember them all today.

Say a little prayer, and remember them for a moment, for love's dear sake.

Because, as someone has well said:

"What is love, but remembering?"

The Obsequious Gentleman and the Babe

We awoke early. Slender spears of golden light were thrusting through the green world outside our window. The crepe myrtle on the edge of the circular garden still smoldered pinkly in emerald shadow. The cool wind shook the leaves of the trees impatiently, but otherwise there was stillness and silence, the echoed silence of the recently departed night. Indeed, the only sounds we heard were the clashing of the leaves and the distant plaintive whistle of the mourning dove.

Afternoon would bring heat, but it would be the reflective heat of late summer, with the countryside full of the sad sweet fragrance of drying hay and grass.

The feel of fall was in the air, and we knew with certainty that the year had passed its zenith and had begun the curving descent into winter and the time of mortality.

It was Stephen Vincent Benet who wrote the poem containing the words:

"And Death, the obsequious gentleman,

Comes rubbing black gloves and talking."

You recall that Benet himself was paid a visit by this obsequious gentleman some 10 years past and thus we suffered the untimely loss of one of the clearest voices of our age.

Just over a week ago we read in the paper that Mildred Didrickson Zaharias, known as "Babe," had received an announcement of an impending visit from this same obsequious gentleman.

It was only a few weeks before that we had finished reading the final chapter of Babe Zaharias' story in the Saturday Evening Post. The last installment was termed "How I Battled Cancer." You recall that several years ago Babe was found to be suffering from a malignancy. She was operated on, an operation that is called a colostomy. It is a drastic operation—if you don't think so, look it up in the encyclopedia.

After the operation, she came back to play golf again—even championship golf.

Now it develops that a pain in her spine is caused by the presence of cancer cells there. Apparently there is nothing that can be done about it. It is just a matter of time.

The Babe's comment was typical. She was quoted as saying: "Well, that's the rub of the green."

Someone else expressed the same idea in the words: "It's just the way the ball bounces,"

The Babe's calm fortitude under the circumstances reminds us of the other Babe—the immortal George Herman Ruth, and also of his heroic teammate, Lou Gehrig, the Iron Man of the New York Yankees.

We have often wondered how we would feel if we received one of these notices from the obsequious gentleman. One never knows, we suppose.

One thing is certain: The world would appear to us in a different light. Each dawn, each sunset, each blade of grass, would have a new significance. The color and the sound and the smell of the earth would take on a new aspect, a different relativity. We would be more apt, as Shakespeare puts it, "To love that well which thou must leave ere long."

Is it not a strange thing that we of mankind, all of whom are born to die, should have so great a fear of mortality? Surely, if our Christian faith means anything, it means that Death is only one more incident in the immortal life of the soul.

We keep thinking of a story we heard years ago. A group of young people were floating down a long winding river on a raft. Finally, one day they heard dimly and far away, a roaring sound. Upon inquiry as to the cause of the sound, they were told that is was the roar of a great waterfall over which their river passed and over which they, too, must pass. The waterfall was called Death.

From that time on, the sound of the falls grew louder in their ears.

How typical this is of our course through life. When we are young, we are so intent upon the sensuous impressions of our ever-expanding horizons that we give no thought to death. But after a certain age, the sound of the falls becomes apparent, and thereafter we seldom lose that sound.

We wonder how many of you have ever seen a magnificient golfer like the Babe hit a golf ball. Angular, lean, tough-muscled, and with a champion's heart, she is a long-hitter. There is the rifle-sharp "crack" as the club head meets the ball and the tiny white sphere takes off as though jet-propelled. It streaks along low and close to the ground and then it begins to rise up, up into the thin air until at last is almost seems to pause and hang motionless for a split second before it falls to the fairway, hundreds of yards away. There is the feel, the ecstasy of flight. A small part of your heart has taken wings and flown with the ball.

That is the kind of thing that the Babe loved and still loves. She hates to contemplate leaving it—and leaving her lovable roly-poly husband, ex-wrestler George Zaharias.

But like Cyrano de Bergerac, that grand swordsman with the big nose and the ugly face, she refuses to be intimidated by the obsequious gentleman, Death. You recall Cyrano's words as he faced the same gentleman:

"I can see him there—he grins—

He is looking at my nose—that skeleton!

What's that you say? Hopeless? Why, very well!

But a man does not fight merely to win!

No-no—better to know one fights in vain! . . ."

To the Babe and to all others who are expecting a visit from the obsequious gentleman, our hearts go out in gratitude and love—gratitude and love for a spirit that "does not fight merely to win," but that demonstrates the heroic quality of man's soul.

And in the Book of Common Prayer there is one particular prayer that has special poignancy and depth for such times:

"O Lord, support us all the day long, until the shadows lengthen and the evening comes, and the busy world is hushed, and the fever of life is over, and our work is done. Then in thy mercy grant us a safe lodging, and a holy rest, and peace at the last. Amen."

Of Dust and Heroes

The Farmers' Market, sometimes called the Curb Market, is a wondrous place, especially early in the morning. The fruits and vegetables are like fabulous jewels; the yellow tasseled corn in its green coat; the scarlet blurt of the tomatoes; the purple of grapes; the red of apples; the yellow and red and pink of the fragrant peaches; and the dark heavy green of the watermelons, and an opened one showing its sweet juicy red meat all dotted with black seed.

There is coolness of the morning, stirring clean and fresh, and overhead the sky flowers like a bright blue morning-glory, all dewy and radiant in the early sun. The earth is magic, and the seasons thereof stir us with emotions that change shimmeringly as water changes when the wind blows over it.

Beyond the market, past the city with its steel and concrete and the stench of its traffic and the sterility of its treeless sidewalks, lies the country—the rolling hills, the green valleys, the mountains shouldering up the sky.

There is the earth—the true earth. There is the dust that God used to make man—the dust to which we all return, willy-nilly. And sometimes, when we contemplate the sorry mess that man can make of his handful of years, we don't feel so badly about the prospect of return to that primal state.

Yet from this same dust come our heroes as well as our failures.

And who has not heroes? Surely there is no soul so dead, no spirit so poverty-stricken, as to not have pictures hung in the gallery of its inmost being—the picture of those fellow creatures who stirred a nameless exultation, or wonder , or love. Whether that picture be of Elvis Presley (Heaven forbid!) or of Ted Williams or of Winston Churchill— it is nonetheless one of the most important possessions of its owner's life.

For, as your heroes are, so will you likely be. And in this life where so much depends on a proper sense of values, yours will be based principally upon those values represented by your heroes.

One of the most rewarding results of reading (which we devoutly hope is not being destroyed by the spoonfed culture of TV and radio) is

99

the chance encounter we have with unexpected and lasting heroes. We cherish the portraits hung at an early age in our heart of hearts: Horatius and his bitter and desperate battle to defend his beloved Rome; Robin Hood, the gay, greenclad daredevil of Sherwood Forest; D'Artagnan, that small, brave and incredibly talented swordsman; and Sherlock Holmes, keen, philosophical, pitting his mind and heart repeatedly against the problems that people brought him, until, miraculously, he broke through.

But all our heroes have not been found in books. One of our favorites was George Bothner, for nearly two decades the undefeated lightweight wrestling champion of the world. Another was Lou Gehrig, who knew how to live greatly, to play baseball more greatly, and to die most greatly. Thomas Wolfe and Steve Benet—oh, there we are back in books again! But these were not in the books—they wrote them!

As we grow older, of course, we change—our tastes, our ideas, our dreams, and aspirations. And while we don't take down the pictures that we have hung, we do hang new ones—and are apt to spend more of our time looking at them than at the others.

In recent years, one of our favorites has been Arthur T. Vanderbilt, who died a few months ago. He was Chief Justice of the Supreme Court of New Jersey. He was a great man—a fighter, a crusader, and withal, a "gentle knight." Now he is dust.

Another, in a different way, was a young man named John Meyer, who died only last week. He was an insurance man, and a fine one. For years he had quite a time with diabetes. He was not strong or robust or even in good health—yet he did a magnificent job as president of the local Jaycees, in his chosen work, and in his beloved Lutheran Church, and with his fine family. And never, ever, did we ever know him to complain. Always he wore a smile. His smile was the bright badge of his courage. Now he, too, is gone.

It is inevitable that others will be going. The way of life is the way of death. Even the indestructible Winston Churchill, whose magnificently thrilling voice uttered the steel-ringing words that saved our free world from destruction—even he will soon be summoned to Valhalla.

But heroes never really die, of course. Oh, yes, they return to the dust—that is, their bodies do. They become part of the April rain—the August corn, stirring in the hot sun—the wine-sweet air of October, when motley leaves are falling—and the frozen sleep of snowy winter. But they are not dead.

The pictures still hang in the hearts.

Who can forget brave Achilles?

Robert the Bruce still lives in vivid reality in the heart of Scotland.

Peter Marshall's glowing words (in Scottish accent!) still sound down the corridors of time.

Babe Ruth still points into center field to show the jeering crowd where he will belt the next ball.

Colin Kelley still swoops through the deathless air. (Do you remember? Look! There hangs his picture!)

John Donne once wrote:

"Death, be not proud, though some have called thee
Mighty and dreadful, for thou art not so;
For those, whom thou think'st thou dost overthrow,
Die not, poor Death, nor yet canst thou kill me.
From rest and sleep, which but thy pictures be,
Much pleasure, then from thee much more must flow;
And soonest our best men with thee do go.
Thou 'rt slave to Fate, Chance, kings, and desperate men,
And dost with poison, war, and sickness dwell,
And poppy or charms can make us sleep as well,
And better than thy stroke, why swell'st thou then?
One short sleep past, we wake eternally.
And Death shall be no more; Death, thou shalt die."

And now, as time flows on and grasses dry in the heat and we smell their mortal fragrance, and as the nights lengthen and the mystic change of the season is again at hand—remember the dust and the heroes.

And, in remembering, your own spirit will be touched with magic, and you will find that the golden coins of your days will acquire a new lustre and will buy more that is worthwhile at the curb market of life.

The Pursuit of Significance

In the November issue of *Country Life* there was a book review of Lewis Mumford's "The Myth of the Machine." In it the reviewer, Geoffrey Grigson, quotes a phrase used by Mumford: "the pursuit of significance."

Not for a long time has a more telling phrase been coined. "The pursuit of happiness" isn't even in the same class with it. After all, most of us have long since learned that to pursue happiness is to never achieve it, for it is, by its very nature, a by-product.

But surely one of the common denominators of being a part of the human race—along with being born, breathing, exulting, loneliness and dying—is the pursuit of significance.

Isn't one of the marks of a great newspaper editor his ability to inspire people to pursue significance?

Many of us have a special regard for Alfred Mynders because of his incalculable contribution along this line through the years.

Long-time editor of the *Times,* and now editor emeritus, Alfred, prior to his *Times* days, was associate editor of the old *Chattanooga News.* He was also secretary of the YMCA for many years, and has been active in every endeavor for the betterment of our area and our nation.

At present, he is recovering from a broken shoulder recently incurred in a traffic accident, and his many friends are pulling for a rapid mending.

Especially do we remember a column that Alfred once wrote years ago about Joan of Arc who was burned at the stake by order of the bishop of Beauvais.

After the bishop's own death, when he went to the afterworld those there prepared to try him for his monstrous cruelty in having Joan executed.

Bur they could find no one who would appear in his defense—and he must have a spokesman in his behalf.

Apparently every one was so embittered toward him that none would assume the role of his advocate.

Then, of a sudden, there was a stirring in the crowd, and a young peasant girl pushed her way to the front and spoke in a clear fresh voice:

"I will defend my lord the bishop," she said.

And the crowd's heart stood still as they gasped in amazement—for the girl was none other than the Maid or Orleans herself—Joan!

In his personal column, "Next to the News," Alfred Mynders spoke to the heart as well as to the head.

Always and ever, he believed, and still believes, in the importance of one's dreams, one's aspirations. The vision should always outrun the reach, he said—and poetry was frequently the medium he used to stir the hearts of his readers.

It was in his column that we first saw:

"Across the fields of yesterday
he sometimes comes to me,
a little lad just back from play
—the lad I used to be.

And yet he smiles so wistfully,
once he has crept within—
I wonder if he hoped to see
the man I might have been!"

Like many of us, Alfred has always been a lover of England and the men who made England great. None who read it will ever forget his column written during the Battle of Britain when he reminded us of the Battle of Waterloo—and the way that Napoleon's dream was shattered as the men of England responded to the challenge: "Stand up, Guards!"

Churchill was one of his heroes. (Quite an inspirational one himself, wasn't he?)

Rudyard Kipling is in the discard now, in this age of anti-colonialism and anti-authority, but the world will come again to the simple verities of much that he said. How timely today is his challenge to the Responsible Man to take up his burden

"And reap his old reward:
The blame of those ye better,
The hate of those ye guard—
The cry of hosts ye humour
(Ah, slowly!) toward the light:
'Why brought ye us from bondage,
Our loved Egyptian night?'"

The transition from ignorance and bondage to maturity and understanding and responsibility is a painful and frequently frustrating one—no matter what one's background. Today, indeed, the irresponsibility of the affluent competes with that of their opposites.

Motivation is hard to engender in either extreme. For motivation must come from within—and there is little of the sort of inspiration that is needed to blow the fire aflame. Perhaps we have forgotten Kipling's:

"Oh Adam was a gardener, and God who made him sees
That half a proper gardener's work is done upon his knees."

Maybe we should go back to some of the old precepts that were in the copybooks studied by school children a century ago. As Kipling pointed out, they always seem to become relevant again:

"As it will be in the future, it was at the birth of Man—
There are only four things certain since Social Progress began:
That the Dog returns to his Vomit, and the Sow returns to her Mire,
And the burnt Fool's bandaged finger goes wobbling back to the
    Fire;
And that after this is accomplished, and the brave new world begins
When all men are paid for existing, and no man must pay for his
    sins,
As surely as Water will wet us, as surely as Fire will burn,
The Gods of the Copybook Headings
With terror and slaughter return!"

But these words are time-rusted and are lost in the blowing of new winds that have risen.

Yet—are they really lost?

It is a wintry day. The snow lies deep and the tangled skein of tree branches is etched black upon a pearl gray sky.

But there are still hearts that glow, that respond to the Keepers of the Flame. And they are the ones, Alfred Mynders, who reach out to you in appreciation and love and gratitude for what you have been and are and will be:

One who has pursued—and achieved—significance!

L'Envoi

When we woke that Thursday morning, it was grey pre-dawn, the air dank and chill. But March is fey, unpredictable, and extravagant—and in an hour's time a heavy snow was falling, huge soft flakes that loaded the trees and the shrubs and spread a white comforter across the raw winter-bitten earth.

It continued to snow, hour after hour. Outside the windows the black and barren trees were clad in ermine, cap-a-pie, as the wintry deluge continued to sift down from the foggy sky.

And so instead of bundling ourselves up and driving off to town, we sat listening to the silent music of the snowy morning and thinking about our friend Alfred Mynders.

Alfred had died the night before. His health had been failing for the past several years.

Virtually blind as he reached the end of his life, he knew better than most the aching loneliness of man, the pitiless lucidity of those black midnight hours.

Perhaps because of that, there were and are many who loved him—even among those who knew him only through his columns and his editorials.

The poet Yeats wrote:

"Words alone are certain good . . .

The wandering earth herself may be

Only a sudden flaming word."

And Alfred had a gift with words. He could paint pictures—not just still-life, but pictures of action, bright with emotion and music.

His columns speak more eloquently of his gift than anything anyone else could say.

As many know, he was always interested in dogs. In one of his last columns, he spoke of Penny, his fox terrier:

"Penny, the lovely fox terrier, has been a wonderful watchdog for the writer, who has a loss of eyesight. Penny listens for her master's voice during the daytime, and at night listens also for any movement from outside that would seem to indicate danger of intrusion into the apartment. And Penny's bark is loud and strong, and would frighten even Jesse James away.

Well, the writer was petting Phoebe, the Dalmatian, and Penny came up and tried with her nose to transfer the writer's pat from Phoebe's head to her own.

Penny's eyes showed devotion

A few tears came down the writer's cheek. Didn't some great poet write an elegy on the death of Keats, which indicated that men may weep?

"I weep for Adonais, he is dead,
Oh weep for Adonais, though
our tears thaw not
The frost which binds so dear
a head."

Well, a few tears can express pride and affection, and that is how the writer feels about Penny, faithful and devoted friend.

As for Penny, an English poet wrote lines to his pet:
"The curate says you have no soul;
I know that he has none . . ."
And it goes on to the end
"When I have crossed to the Promised land
I know your leaping ghost will
Leap to lick my phantom hand."

We are sure that when Alfred entered the great halls of heaven, the first to spy him and greet him with delight would be his four-legged friends who had gone before!

And though Alfred was, withal, a gentle man, he had a fierce undying courage.

He had been in the infantry in France in World War I, and he knew that there are things worth dying for, just as there are things worth living for.

In the early days of World War II when England was embattled and it appeared that all was lost, he wrote a magnificent column in which he recalled the way that English courage had turned defeat into victory in the Battle of Waterloo. The following is quoted from it:

"The supreme moment was at hand. Napoleon, his army buckling all about him, his star already in eclipse, had launched the Imperial Guard, his pride, at Wellington's center. The catapult was coming * * * Crouched for the flash, the red-coated regiments of the Duke fixed their eyes on the little rise in front. Already the ground under them trembled with the headlong rush of the French echelons * * * Closer and closer—a stri-

106

dent din—a terrifying clamor of galloping horses and shouting men. Then the tall hats of the first of the charging grenadiers, only 50 yards away. * * * Were these fighting giants still invincible? Many a bloody field bore the marks of their devastation. The steaming nostrils of those splendid war steeds were plain—the magnificent muscles of their heaving chests—

"Stand up! Guards!"

That short command from Wellington ended Waterloo. English bullets riddled the dashing ranks; English steadiness and courage were like granite. The catapult was stopped * * * the June sun sank—and with it the splendor of Napoleon."

It was not long after that column was written that Winston Churchill stood up in the House of Commons and flung the challenge that kindled a spark in the hearts of Englishmen and of all free men everywhere in his flaming gesture of defiance at the time of the Battle of Dunkirk—and again, by the force of spirit, defeat was turned into victory.

The final quotation is from a column Alfred wrote in 1938. It was a tribute to James Weldon Johnson:

"The death of James Weldon Johnson in a grade-crossing accident in Maine on June 26 brought to close one of the most distinguished careers in the history of the Negro in America.

"Editorials in the leading Eastern newspapers have extolled his achievements as a teacher and professor, a member of the consular service, a writer of songs that have been on everyone's tongue, editor of the music and poetry of the Negro, high-minded public leader in the affairs of his race, poet, and author of several widely known books. His own story was told in his autobiography, "Along This Way."

"It is significant that James Weldon Johnson asked to have buried with him a copy of his own favorite among his books, "God's Trombones," seven of the old-time Negro sermons which he set into enduring verse. One of these poems, given below, seems particularly appropriate at this time and is published here with the express permission of the Viking Press, owners of the copyright:

"'GO DOWN DEATH—A Funeral Sermon

Weep not, weep not,
She is not dead;
She's resting in the bosom of Jesus.
Heartbroken husband—weep no more;
Grief-stricken son—weep no more;
Left-lonesome daughter—weep no more;

She's only just gone home.

107

Day before yesterday morning,
God was looking down from his great, high heaven
Looking down on all his children,
And his eye fell on Sister Caroline
Tossing on her bed of pain
And God's big heart was touched with pity,
With the everlasting pity.
And God sat back on his throne,
And he commanded that tall, bright angel standing at his right hand:
Call me Death!
And that tall, bright angel cried in a voice
That broke like a clap of thunder:
Call Death!—Call Death!
And the echo sounded the streets of heaven
Till it reached way back to that shadowy place,
Where Death waits with his pale white horses.
                 * * *

And God said: Go down, Death, go down
Go down to Savannah, Georgia,
Down in Yamacraw,
And find Sister Caroline.
                 * * *

And Death took her up like a baby.
And she lay in his icy arms,
But she didn't feel no chill.
And Death began to ride again—
Up beyond the evening star,
Out beyond the morning star.
Into the glittering light of glory,
On to the Great White Throne.
And there he laid Sister Caroline
On the loving breast of Jesus,
And Jesus took his own hand and wiped away her tears,
And he smoothed the furrows from her face,
And the angels sang a little song.
And Jesus rocked her in His arms,
And kept a-saying: Take your rest,
Take your rest, take your rest."

Alfred was buried in the National Cemetery. It was a lovely day of
late winter or early spring, the high arching sky as blue as the robin's
egg. The great trees in the cemetery, twiggy and bare, leaned quiet on

the chilly air, and the white headstones stood in ordered ranks across the green grass.

And so Alfred, too, will take his rest and will sleep a while.

But it is Kipling who can express best how so many of us feel as to what will ultimately happen:

"When earth's last picture is painted, and the tubes are twisted and dried,

When the oldest colors have faded, and the youngest critic has died,

We shall rest, and, faith, we shall need it—lie down for an aeon or two,

Till the Master of All Good Workmen shall set us to work anew!" . . . .

Hasta pronto, amigo!

The Last of September

*"Now is the bitter season of the year
When dying summer brings her fruits to ground."*
                                    —Robert Nathan

It is the last of September.

The feel of fall is in the air, and yet, betimes, the sun blazes as clanging fierce as in July. But the lushness is gone. There is dryness in the grass and leaves and even in the throat, and the dogwood berries are as scarlet as tiny drops of blood.

This year more than any before there is a note of bittersweet nostalgia, of homesickness and mortality that stabs our hearts even as we are pierced by the poignant scent of drying grasses and the subtle sweet smell of apples and the wistful fragrance of the leaves that are already beginning to turn.

Why do we have this unusual sense of mortality?

There may be several reasons.

First, we ourselves are not so young as we have been.

Someone has said that life's journey is like riding on a raft that drifts down a river. At the beginning there is only the joy and the freshness: the golden sunlight spinning its magic web; the dew glittering like diamonds on the green leaves that overhang the stream; the glad sweet singing of the birds, their music trembling on the morning air; and the youthful heart full of the anguish and ecstasy of high adventure.

But then, suddenly, one day we become conscious of a sound—dim and fade away—but nonetheless, a definite sound. It is a dull murmur as of distant thunder, almost imperceptible, yet surely there. And when we inquire as to the nature of it, we are told that it is the roar of the great falls far down the river over which one day we must pass—and the name of the falls is Death.

At first, we are silent, troubled. But soon we forget and life again is gay and carefree. But the sound remains, and little by little it grows louder until one day we notice it again. And this time it is not mere background, but is imminent, more nearer, and we realize that much of our journey is done, and that we must be careful as to how we spend the time that remains.

So perhaps one reason that we are more conscious this year of this chill that touches our heart as summer ends is that we realize that time has spun away, the golden days have dropped like petals into the dark waters of the river. There is a sense of impending loss, of separation, of mortality.

But there is more.

Another and even stronger reason is exemplified by Marion Peck's magnificent story in last Sunday's *Times* on the subject of the exceptional child.

It is most discouraging that at this moment in world history when our Western civilization desperately needs its highest degree of excellence, we are deliberately downgrading ourselves by a soft-headed, soft-hearted and mistaken insistence upon equality among people of various races.

The truth of the matter is that race, per se, has little or nothing to do with equality or inequality. That is an individual matter.

We do not insist upon equality among members of our own race. Why, then, do we stubbornly contend that we must accord equality to those of another race simply because they are of another race?

Instead of destroying the potential excellence of our nation by downgrading our entire school system to protect the "less privileged"—(which is our kindly description of the less capable)—why do we not practice segregation by ability, and keep our best talent alive and growing so that we may face the challenge of the present and the future?

Otherwise we will be like the lemmings, those peculiar little animals that periodically make a madly concerted dash to the sea into which they plunge themselves and drown.

Excellence and equality are antithetical. This is a hard but no less real fact. The one spells survival, and the other annihilation.

Which way will we take?

There is a third reason for our more than normally heavy sense of mortality.

An individual, like a nation, creates an image in the mind and the eye of others.

On the basis of that image, the observer either respects or disrespects, likes or dislikes, fears or does not fear, that person.

What has happened to the image of the United States of America?

Have we lost that quality that made others respect us, like us or fear us, somewhere along the road which we have mistakenly called progress?

Have we indeed, as suggested by Sen. Margaret Chase Smith, lost our national will to risk everything for our beliefs?

Perhaps it is true, as James Reston suggests, that our President has talked like Churchill and acted like Chamberlain.

In any event, the spirit of the people of the United States demands a more decisive attitude. As someone has well put it, to stand forever at the crossroads is more than flesh and blood can endure.

And surely it requires but a modicum of common sense to know that friendship cannot be bought, and that fawning, cringing, grovelling and embracing as "equals" those whose veneer of civilization is not even paper-thick, does nothing to improve our national image.

Montgomery of Alamein may have been right in his recent book, "The Path to Leadership," when he declared that the failure of the United States to maintain world stature is due to our childish insistence on being loved and on wanting everyone to like us in all we do.

As parents, as individuals, we know the fallacy of that approach.

Somehow, some way, we must change. We must declare ourselves --our beliefs, our position, and our attitude. We can still be friendly or helpful, but on our own terms. And if others don't like that, they will simply have to make the most of it.

What Washington and President Kennedy do not know is that the people of the United States are much more willing to sacrifice than their political leaders are willing to ask them to sacrifice.

What Washington and President Kennedy and the world need to know is that we people of the United States of America are a God-fearing and justice-loving people, but that there are certain basic principles that we must insist upon—to the death, if need be.

Each of us know that some day we will pass over the falls down the river. That much is certain. Death cannot be escaped.

But we can decide how we will die—whether it will be bravely or whether, on the contrary, it will be cowardly, rottenly, screaming and kicking.

Those of us who were fortunate enough to be brought up in the era before television and radio may remember our parents reading to us those lines from Macaulay's "Lays of Ancient Rome":

"Then out spake brave Horatius,
        The Captain of the Gate:
'To every man upon this earth
        Death cometh soon or late.
And how can man die better
        Than facing fearful odds,
For the ashes of his fathers,
        And the temples of his gods?'"

And so, in this mortal season when we are touched with the sadness of autumn and of summer gone, let us renew our contact with the basic principles and the sound ideals that make for liberty and rewrite upon the tablets of our hearts our pledge of life and death and sacred honor.

Then and then only can we look forward with equanimity and confidence to either life or death, and the bitterness of the season fades and is gone. For our conscience will be clear—and as we all know, it is only when we are at peace with ourselves that life means anything, anyway.

1960 - 1990

The Golden Spell

Dark rain fell heavily that first night,
   And water ran from the roof
And the gutters, and the ground was soggy—
   Swill-full, mucky to the touch.
And we sat before the flame-flattering fire in the snugness,
   Feeling the warmth of our drinks
And the warmth of our comradeship
   While outside the cold rain fell on and on
In the blackness of the February night.
   And when we went to sleep,
It was to the dark music of the rain.
   But the next day—oh that was different!
The sun swam up into the clear blue sky,
   And all the birds in all the world were singing
As though their hearts overflowed
   With the ecstasy and beauty of the earth!
Even the naked trees,
   All twigged with branches in the blue bright air,
Were lacquered in the golden wash
   Of the sunlight, and the chill wind
Was flooded with the sun rays
   That warmed the body and the heart and the soul.
And the glowing flame of the camellias
   Heated the eye, and the hearts of all of us
Rose, swelling balloonlike as the sun rose
   Higher and higher.

We left in a green jeep,
   With the dogs penned in their box
In the back, and we drove
Along red clay roads, still mucky,
   Rill-brimming and
   Chocked with holes full of shining water,
Alongside pastures where cattle stood,

Lifting their heads to stare curiously at us
As we passed. And then
    We came to a gate, and opening it
    Drove through
And along the side of a field.
    The grass of the field was grey
Like the short stubbly beard
    Of an old man, and the bare trees
Were spikey like unkempt hair.
    The wind blew and it was cold,
But the warmth of the sun came through and fought the cold.
    We heard frogs creaking in the boggy places,
And we could smell the rank
    Fermented smell of the silage that the cattle
Eat in winter, and we could hear the
    Blowing sound of the wind in the pine trees.

Finally, lurching and bumping along, we came
    To a wire fence. Alex and Enzo climbed down
Off the jeep and drew their guns from their
    Scabbards, and Parker on horseback was handling the dogs
Who tumbled out of their box and began to
    Range, running, leaping high in the tall grass.
Circling and looking and scenting; and now they were
    All on the other side of the fence, and they
Began to walk through the briars and sage grass
    And among the little pine trees and I stayed
At the jeep, leaning against the side of it,
    Drowsy in the sun, feeling the heat of the sunlight
And full of sweet pleasure and wonder for the mere
    Being alive on such a day.

Then, of a sudden,
    They had stopped . . . and were frozen like statues.
The dogs were pointing—still as still,
    Their nostrils aquiver, their heads low.
Enzo and Alex held their guns at the ready.
    Half a mile away, a tractor was going by on a dirt road,
But its noise was like nothing—it was
    Ignored, it was a different world. And
Then Parker moved forward, and the birds
    Roared up like thunder out of the briary bush

And the air was filled with their wings and
   The noise of their jagged flight—and the guns
Fired and fired again, and the covey was
   Gone into the trees and the bushes and the   '
Dogs were leaping. There were four
   Dead quail. They lay still and graceful,
The sunlight warm on their feathers.

When death comes sudden and quick
   There is an almost beauty to it.
Perhaps we're envious—who knows?—
   We who fear age and decay—who fear
The loss of the vibrancy, the urgency, the
   Sweetness of life. And so we go
Tramping the woods and fields,
   Scorning the briars, slogging through mud
And tangled thickets, up hill, down dale,
   To carry this small message of mortality—
Or is it immortality?

And so that day we went—pausing for lunch—
   Then traveling to other fields.
The jeep plows through the sea
   Of tattered cornstalks, and the dry dust flies
In upon us. The dogs lope back and forth,
   Circling, searching. Then of a sudden,
Parker, atop his horse, raises his hand—
The dogs have stopped again.
There in the grass they scent the
   Hidden partridge. This time Clay
Moves in—the whir of wings
   Explodes—his gun fires twice—
Then Alex's—Walter's too—
   Some hit . . . some miss.
But time swings on, and
   Bird by bird, we add until as
Darkness nears, we have twenty
   Quail or more. A good days shoot.
And when the sun goes down
   And purple dusk flowers like a secret rose
And blooms upon the earth,

Before the stars can trim their tiny lamps,
We journey homeward. Tired and quite relaxed,
    We watch the sunset colors fade and drain
Out of the western sky.
Atop a hill
We pass an old deserted farmhouse gray with age,
    Where nearby stands a lofty-towered windmill, dark
Against the dark blue sky.
    In the breeze the windmill turns
Around, around, around. And though
    It's not connected, and its turning does
No work, it still must turn.

As so must we.
The dogs are tired and we
    Climbing, bone-weary from the
Mud-caked jeep, go in to
    Take hot steamy baths, then have a drink, then eat—
And sleep.

It's been a day to long remember.

But what is printed strongest
    On our hearts
Is this: Today was good—
    We spent ourselves—some birds
Were gotten and some lost. But
    Most of all: Tomorrow is another day.
And so we fall asleep, rocked in
    The golden spell of our anticipation.
And that's the best of all.

The Needle of Noon

Chamonix, France—There's a strange magic in the way that one night you're in New York in the glut of traffic, the blazing lights, hearing and feeling the heavy pulse of the city's life, the trembling of the street when the subway roars by beneath you—and then, taking off on a SwissAir jet, you thunder out into the darkness, eat dinner, cat-nap, then wake to watch the stars pale and vanish as the dawn flares up the eastern sky, and you coast down through the puffy white clouds and glide to a perfect landing at Geneva.

The summer has been a wet, cold one for Europe, and the wetness lingers on. The first day it rained most of the time—a fine, misty rain much like you find in Ireland, when they say "It's a soft day." We walked miles and miles through the old part of the city, visiting the huge marble Monument De la Reformation, shopping, and then catching a bus out to the Perle du Lac, a world-famous restaurant located in a park that was formerly a private estate. The restaurant is housed in what was a combination guesthouse and stable. The bisque de homard — lobster cream soup—was only the beginning of an epicure's delight.

At the next table was a quintet of Egyptians connected with either the U.N. or the International Labor Office that headquarters in Geneva— and one of them was the most sinister looking person we've ever seen. He would flash a smile and then his face would relapse into a cold mask of dedicated and implacable harshness.

We taxied home to the Hotel Beau Rivage and slept like logs.

But the next day was the one. Never have we had anything like it.

It was the day we went to Chamonix and took the cable car to the Aiguille du Midi—"The Needle of Noon."

We gathered at 8:30 at the square where the buses park, and departed—practically a whole busload. It was a grey chilly morning, and as we drove out of the city and through the green valleys toward Chamonix, rain fell, and our spirits fell with it. At Chamonix the bus unloaded near the cable car station. We could see the cables stretching steeply up the mountainside and disappearing in the blowing clouds.

Most of our fellow travelers went immediately in to buy their tickets and catch the next cable car, but we wandered off down a little street and bought some bread and cheese and wine, and it must have been forty minutes before we began the ride.

It was crowded in the cable car, most of the passengers were German or French, and there was much exclamation in many tongues as we started our swaying, lurching ride.

The valley fell away with startling swiftness, and as we reached the end of the first stage and changed to another car, we noted that the car had coldened appreciably. By the time we were some five or six thousand feet up the little town of Chamonix looked tiny and far away.

Just after starting the second stage, we entered the clouds and were lost in a world of cold blowing mists, being dragged by a spider's line to an unknown and giddy destination. Occasionally we could glimpse jagged grey rocks below us through the clouds, and at last, with sleet rattling loudly on the roof of our car, we were hauled almost vertically up a dark cliff face into a small station that was lashed to the rock by metal cables.

We were now up to almost thirteen thousand feet, and as we climbed the icy steps to the heated waiting room above, we felt the altitude. We were short of breath and somewhat faint. Peering out the windows, we could see nothing at all save the wind-whipped clouds and occasional spatterings of snow, and the long icicles that hung from the eaves.

So it was that we decided to ride the next car down, and felt a derisive bitterness at anyone's stupidity for being lured into this tourist trap. We each got a cup of hot coffee, and it was then that I left the others and climbed the ice-coated stairs to the top platform—it was open—uncovered—and the wind blew like a witch's gale, and the snow bit at my face and the roaring of the wind filled my ears.

Then suddenly it happened: there was a growing luminosity, and after several seconds the clouds blew away and I was standing in brilliant sunlight, over two miles high in a blue sky atop a needle of rock! On every side snowy peaks towered against the sky, and far, far below lay the green valleys and the tiny village of the world we left behind.

Hurrying back down the steep slippery steps, I fetched the others, and we came up again, and stood and felt our hearts soar and swoop, and when a jet flew overhead drawing its long vapor trail behind it, we felt ourselves the equal—even the superior—of the people flying in it. After all, they were snug and warm in a pressurized cabin, while we were (albeit clothed) naked in the wind!

The blue of the air, the piercing brilliance of the light, the sound of the wind, the whiteness of the snow—all these wove a magic web in which our hearts were snared and from which we shall never be entirely free.

And so we ate our lunch, sitting in the waiting room, and peering out the windows into the sun-glittering air—and our hearts were filled with delight and surprise, as there we sat, thrust miles up into the sky atop "The Needle of Noon." And there was the spice of fear in the flavor of that time, for we felt the huge aching pull of the depth, and thought of the brave men who had climbed this rocky spire with ice axe and piton and rope and had made fast the cables that our very lives depended on.

Afterward, there was no way to go but down.

Which is, we suppose, the lesson taught by all achievement—whether it be that of a person, a society, or any other living thing.

We have never felt that lesson so poignantly, so piercingly as when there.

But there are always other heights to challenge us!

Londonderry Air

Oh, Danny boy, the pipes, the pipes are calling
From glen to glen, and down the mountainside,
The summer's gone, and all the roses falling,
It's you, it's you must go, and I must bide.

There's a magic about Ireland that tugs at the heart. We were there again in September and October, and again there was its poignant autumn beauty, sweet and sad. The green or straw-yellow loveliness of the fields, the softness of the misty rain, the leprechaun-gold of the sunlight, the grey of the ancient crooked stone walls and arched bridges, the subtle, faintly ammoniac smell of the blue-feathered peat smoke— all these were there, and all are a part of the living legend that is Ireland.

Also part of that legend is the openness and courage and friendliness of the Irish people. There is a unique spirit among the Gaelic—you pass a countryman walking along a rural lane, or riding his donkey cart, or pedalling his bicycle, and he greets you with a smile and an upflung hand. There is no subservience, nor superiority, nor inferiority, nor equality nor inequality. He is his own man, and greets you as his own man. How different from most!

Why, then, do we hear of violence and terrorism—of fury and insane killings, of fire and destruction in the Emerald Isle?

Why, indeed?

When we were there a few weeks ago, we talked with friends and with strangers, Irish folk from all walks of life, and came to certain conclusions. Here they are for whatever they are worth:

Man's Nature

The reason for the fighting is that man is a curious combination of contradictions—of good and evil, of strength and weakness, of kindness and blind fury. Despite the preachments of the well-intentioned but shallow-thinking, there are forces and counter-forces in man that whip up emotional storms as deadly and destructive as the tropical storms that blow in out of the Caribbean or that rip through the China Sea.

Sometimes we wonder if the hunger for fighting is not as deeply embedded an instinct as the hunger for food or for love. Certain it is that from time to time, war, which is mass fighting, seizes the body of mankind like a fit of epilepsy and off we careen into violence and counter-violence.

War, or fighting, can be occasioned by any number of diverse and even contradictory things:

. . . religion, race, money, water—even, in the case of the Trojan War, the beauty of a woman's face. Yet in a sense, most of these things were not the reason, but rather the excuse, for the blood letting.

No Good Wars, But . . .

Out of the crucible of conflict there come things good and bad, great and petty, self-sacrificial as well as selfish and intolerant. Those who would oppose war under any circumstance should remember that there are, in truth, things worth fighting for and dying for. It may well be said that while there are no good wars, there are some necessary wars.

In Ireland, the current fighting appears on its face to be due to unfair treatment accorded the Catholic minority by the Protestant majority in the six counties of Northern Ireland. These six counties are a part of the British Commonwealth. The rest of Ireland, some 26 counties, is independent of Britain and constitutes the Republic of Ireland. It is heavily Catholic, and the greatest danger at present is that the Republic of Ireland might send troops into Northern Ireland to help the beleaguered Catholics drive out the British and the Protestants there.

We advisedly say that this appears "on its face" because this is, again, apparently only the excuse for the fighting rather than the reason.

In our own country—even in our own community—we are witnessing the hardening of attitudes and that growing fear that presages conflict. Rudeness and insolence are rampant, and violence has become commonplace.

What can be done about it?

It would appear that the first thing we must do is to recognize and deal with the basic Natural Law that says that man must feel needed. John W. Gardner makes this point strongly in his latest book, "The Recovery of Confidence."

How stupid and wrong we are when we think we can solve the problems of the poor or the black or the young simply by giving them money!

To do that is to let them know that they are not needed—and that makes them hate themselves, and end up by hating the rest of us. We must make demands upon people in exchange for what we give them and thus build their ego and enable them to appreciate themselves and to be appreciated by others.

Another thing we must do is to jettison, once and for all, the false egalitarianism that has been so grotesquely mishandled in recent years. We must recognize individuals as individuals and stop categorizing people. We must remember that people are of varying degrees of maturity, knowledge, wisdom and experience—and that each one acts and reacts on the basis of what is contained within his personal perimeter.

A Force of Unity
When the Mets won the World Series, we happened to be on the telephone with a friend in New York who told how that the people in the city were going wild in celebration. He said he couldn't understand why they acted like that. We suggested that the reason was obvious: New York is a sick city—a confused and chaotic city, splintered by division and bitterness—and the Mets gave everyone there something to identify with, something clean and good and hard-hitting and victorious.

Everyone needs to be able to identify with something. Unfortunately, in this age of non-heroes, there are few opportunities. Too many end up huddling over a TV screen and imagining they are quarterbacks or ends or something—a sort of Walter Mitty dreamworld.

Another thing that we can do and must do is to recognize that we made a mistake in assuming that we will cure our racial problems by forcing people together indiscriminately and insisting upon their compatibility. There is a vast gulf between desegregation on the one hand and forced integration on the other—and the Supreme Court (and many others) appear to have mistakenly assumed that they were the same. Desegregation is a "not forcing;" integration is a "forcing."

This must be corrected—the quicker the better.

Those blacks who wish to be together should be allowed to do so.

Those whites who wish to be together should be allowed to do so.

And the great and more responsible middle group who are willing to accept an individual as an individual and attempt to get along together on that kind of basis should be allowed to do so.

And finally, we must recognize that man can live in a society only if he is subject to a system of rewards and punishments. Both must be present—and must be used.

Leadership Urgent
Where will we find the leadership that has the wisdom and the courage to implement this?

We'd better hurry. It's as though we were in a plane that has gone into a spin and is falling. At the moment it doesn't matter who got the spin started—the important thing is that it be stopped before we all crash, the bad of us along with the good!

And cleverness—even the cleverness of the so-called sophisticates— will not suffice to save us.

The Shining Racer

For the young heart like the spring wind grows cold
And the dust, the shining racer, is overtaking
The laughing young people who are running like fillies
The golden ladies and the rag-pickers
And the foolish companions of spring, the wild wood lilies.
—Edith Sitwell
Green Song

January is the time of mortality and of the intimations of immortality, for it is then that we realize most poignantly that time is indeed a river of no return.

When one is young, the current seems to move so slowly as to be more like a lake than a river, but as one grows older, he becomes increasingly conscious of its gathering speed—especially as one hears the ever-loudening roar of the rapids through which all mankind must pass.

Yet though we may not turn again upstream to those bright meadows and sunny hills by which we came, we may recapture them if we be careful and deft enough. They can be trapped in a net of shining words, a drawn line, a theme of music, a particular perfume or fragrance—even a photograph, especially if it be ill-focused. (And why ill-focused? Because then it has more overtone, and art is art only if it has overtone!)

And even if we are obsessed in this season by our thoughts of mortality, we need to keep in mind that, as Freya Stark puts it:

"Death, too, is an enhancer. Through him life gains its color, clinging precarious like some Alpine flower that digs its tenuous and tenacious roots in the rock face against the darkness of the drop below. The secret joy of peril comes from the veiled presence without which most savor goes; and this is no morbid feeling, for the ecstasy belongs not to death in itself, but to life, suddenly enriched to know itself alive. So, after a summer dawn and climb till noon, among clefts and icy triangles or wind-scooped crannies, the mountaineer returning sets foot again on the short turf and flowers; and the breeze that cools him is the same breeze that sways the harebells; the blood that tramples in his ears and runs

126

like chariots through his veins is the kind, swift, temporary stuff by which the smaller things are fed: he is back in the community of his kind and descends, light-footed, among the pastures; but he remembers how in the high silences he had known himself on the edge of Silence and how its wing has brushed him."

In the past year, we have lost friends, both young and old. The most grievous losses have been the ones we felt to be premature and untimely and unnecessary. Yet even as to them, our grief is mainly a selfish grief—we weep for ourselves, for the loss of those whom we loved and who loved us, and for the taking away of the opportunity for the kindness and affection they gave us, or that we gave them.

And what of the intimations of immortality that haunt this winter season?

We all know we must die. We know it—but we don't think it.

Yet though there is inevitably biological death, what of the metaphysical You—the part that is the true You?

When we see how young even our elders can be, we know that vitality is not a matter of years. Dorothy Saunders remarks that:

"A Greek scholar once told me that the saying 'those whom the gods love die young' would be more correctly translated by 'those whom the gods love die young in heart'; whether he was right I am in no position to judge, knowing no Greek, but certainly the hallmark of a youthful mind is its readiness to accept the new. It is not the octogenarian who reads small prints without his glasses and walks five miles every day who is young for his age; he is often obstinate and pigheaded. It is the frail old chap who listens to the other fellow's point of view, knows what is going on on the other side of the globe, tries some of the new gadgets, and is willing to alter habits channelled by years, it is he who is beloved by the gods."

In November we were in Boston and attended services at Trinity Church, the church of Phillip Brooks who wrote "O Little Town of Bethlehem." In the pews was the printed sermon of the preceding Sunday. It was entitled "Where Are the Dead?" and had been delivered by the Rev. Theodore P. Ferris, rector of the church. He spoke of the superiority of man to machines and to plants and to animals and then went on:

"The relationship between a man's body and his life is a very strange and mysterious one. We shall never come to the final understanding of it. They are intimately joined together in an inseparable union, and yet you have the feeling all the time that a man's life and his body are not completely identical. He rises above it so many times, gets outside of it every time his memory stretches back across the years, every time his imagination looks forward to a vision of the future. And what has impressed me most of all, as I have seen people coming near the end, when the body was wearing out and had almost stopped, the person himself is often going on stronger than ever before, as though he were declaring, My body is not my case; it is my instrument; I am the player and the player and the instrument are not identical. So intimately are his body and his life joined together that you cannot think of one part from the other, yet you cannot think of his body as completely identical with him, himself."

In this January season, especially when we have one of those rather spring-like days with the sun washing the pastel colors of the earth with its pale light, we can almost feel the faint heartbeat of the immortality that lies locked in the ground and the air and in all of space—the heartbeat that is of the immortal side of man, the side that partakes of God.

So why should we fear the shining racer?

For though the river of time flows on, our hearts tell us that ahead and beyond the rapids lie the still waters and the green pastures of which the Psalmist spoke.

Casey Jones and the Ghosts

The engine pulled up at Reno Hill,
Tooted for the crossing, loud and shrill—
The trainmen knew by the engine's moans
That the man at the throttle was Casey Jones.

The first weekend in August we experienced one of the spine-tingling thrills that are the highlights of man's existence.

It was the occasion of the gathering at the Terminal Station of the nearly 1,000 men, women and children who came to ride the eighteen-car train down the TAG line to Gadsden, then back up the West Valley over the Southern tracks, behind a doubleheader of two steam locomotives.

As we drove to the old and virtually abandoned Terminal Station, we were amazed at the scores of automobiles parked there. Finding a spot to park our own car, we walked to the station and out onto the platform.

There, on either side of us were two lines of passenger cars, on adjoining tracks. The last car on the one was an observation car. As we walked on down the platform between the cars and toward the engines up ahead, steam was hissing from the couplings and the people were swarming to and fro. There were Pullman cars, day coaches, baggage cars, a dining car and —miracle of miracles!—even a white-jacketed Pullman porter!

It was a vision out of the past, and a wave of nostalgia hit us.

On and on we walked until we came out from under the shed and there stood the two great locomotives, in tandem. A few minutes later they would move their cars ahead, then back up on the other track, hook onto the other string of cars, and be ready to go.

What a flood of memories came over us!

There were the occasions when our father would drive us children down to Wauhatchie to see the Dixie Flyer pass. Oley Hulse, the engineer, was a friend of his. We would stand some thirty feet back from the track and our father would pull out his watch.

"It's almost time," he'd say.

Soon after, sure enough, we would hear the train coming. It made a dim, wind-softened, trundling sound. Then we would see the locomotive, far off coming down the grade from Whiteside into Wauhatchie Valley. And then, of a sudden, we could see white steam flare from the whistle and seconds later hear the whistle. It was a mournful, troubling, even threatening, sound.

On and on it came, truly flying, as its name proclaimed, until it flashed past us with a thunder of sound, and the wind of its passing would shake the earth—and there in the window of the cab was the goggled face of the engineer, and he lifted his gloved hand and waved to us, and was gone.

Then the roar and the clickity-clack of the cars swept past, and the train dwindled into the distance and disappeared.

But within our hearts, from then on, it was never completely gone.

There were the times, too, when we would ride the train ourselves: the hot cindery day coaches, full of grimy people and with a news butch to sell us warm cold drinks and sandwiches and candy—or the Pullman cars with exotic names, where one could sleep (if one had the money) in a sheeted berth made up by a friendly porter, and wake up in the night to the clickety-clack of the wheels and sometimes find that the train had stopped in a small unknown town—and we would slide the window shade up and look out on a deserted street, feebly lighted and steeped in midnight and loneliness, and wonder where we were and what the people's lives were like who lived there.

The dining cars, too—what an adventure! What fabulous foods graced the fresh-clothed tables! And how miraculous was the balance of the white-jacketed waiters as they bore the trays of delicious viands from the kitchen to the table!

We remember, too, the names of the trains: the Twentieth Century Limited (we remember a painting of two trains passing in a snowstorm, entitled "When the Centuries Pass"!); the Dixie Flyer; the Royal Palm; and the Pan American.

Lying abed at night, a child could hear the far-off whistle in the valley and the sound rose and fell with a melancholy sweetness that wrenched the heart.

What dreams of distant cities they evoked! We could almost see the white towers of those cities soaring into the clean blue of the early morning, stroked by the golden feather of the sunlight, and the great liners and their piers near the harbor mouth, awaiting in majestic splendor the time to cross the trackless furrows of the sea to lands beyond the horizon.

We recall a poem written by an eighteen-year-old—a youth of another and less unsettled age—that spoke of the drama of the train. It was called "Workmen Unseen," and it ended as follows:

"The sun—the moon—they do not see the set face of a grim man-thing clinging on the seat of the bucking cab—squinting along the sweaty sides of the boiler, hand on throttle, to see whether the light be red or green."

Lost in our dreams of yesterday we were suddenly yanked back by the familiar "All Aboa-a-ard!"

The people scrambled up the steps.

There was a hiss of air as the brakes were released.

Then, with a slight shudder, the cars began to move . . .out, out from the station and away.

The people on the platform called and waved good-bye as the train gathered speed and vanished in the distance.

And as we turned back toward the again deserted station, we realized that it was really not deserted at all.

The ghosts are there.

We could see them . . . we could hear them . . . the Royal Palm . . . Old 97 . . . Casey Jones . . . and, after all, aren't the ghosts—the most real of all?

The Lonely Sea and the Sky

It was nearly eight years ago that we came across Sir Francis Chichester's autobiography titled "The Lonely Sea and the Sky." At that time the author had not yet become famous—but anyone who started reading the story of his life found it difficult to put down.

Born just after the turn of the century, he dropped out of school in 1918, and shipped out to New Zealand. Arriving there, he farmed, prospected for gold, and did a bit of boxing.

His first bid for fame was in 1931, when, piloting a fragile single-engine Gypsy Moth, he became the first man to fly alone from England to Australia.

During World War II he served as navigation expert for the RAF—which, ironically, he could not join because of bad eyesight. After the war, he turned his energies toward "mano a mano" combat with the sea.

In 1960, still weak from a near-fatal bout with lung cancer, he won the first single-handed trans-Atlantic yacht race and, 12 months later, beat his own time across to New York by seven days. Again, in 1964, he raced alone across the Atlantic in a yacht designed for a crew of six.

His crowning achievement, though, was in 1966, when he circum-navigated the globe in his custom-built Gypsy Moth IV, stopping only in Sydney, Australia, and rounding Cape Horn as he headed back for England where he was knighted by his Queen.

Now the news is that he is dead.

Well—maybe so.

Maybe not.

Perhaps it is the peculiar flavor of this season that fosters our doubts. The last few days have brought to us the poignant realization that summer is waning. The sun's lessening heat, the spiced smell of dried grasses heavy in the air, the early morning chill which has the cool, sad feel of fall—these and the occasional scarlet leaves that shine like jewels among the green of the trees, stir our hearts. And after one has lived a certain number of years and has repeatedly seen the wheel of time turn down to winter and rise again to springtime, there comes a sort of fatalism coupled with a peculiar kind of disbelief in mortality.

One of our proudest moments was having our picture taken in Plymouth, England, as we stood in front of the pub named the Sir Francis Chichester. In some quirky way it gave us a sense of being a part of that tough-minded, tough-bodied freebooter who saw so many vistas of adventure. In a day when the poor are called the disadvantaged, and the softlings of a decadent society aspire to a workless life, it's a heartening thing to see at least one man of guts and muscle who thumbs his nose at obstacles and dangers and undertakes the impossible to show the superiority of spirit over mere things.

His autobiography "The Lonely Sea and the Sky" is a classic of self-discovery, of self-reliance and of ingenuity. The denouement of that book—when he took off in Japan and rammed into some wires which sprung and hurled his plane and him to the ground—is only one of the many miracles that have marked his checkered career.

The high point of the story of his world-circling voyage, titled "Gypsy Moth Circles the World," was his rounding the Horn. In that grim place of bitter cold, of giant spume-capped seas and lashing winds, of driving snow and vicious rocky islands, his tiny craft nearly foundered and went under.

But it didn't . . . it didn't. The sheer raw courage of its captain-crew kept it going.

And to read his account of that long lonesome journey is to understand a bit of what has brought man from the Stone Age into the modern world a world that now appears likely to be destroyed by a curious combination of success and irresponsibility.

Francis Chichester, of course, was no ordinary man.

As late as this very summer, he entered a transAtlantic race for one-man craft from England to America. But this time he had to forfeit: malignancy of the spine forced him to conclude that he might well become completely incapacitated in the course of the voyage, and he feared that his craft might then become a menace to others in the race.

So he turned back.

But only temporarily, you may be sure.

A spirit such as his reminds us of Churchill and the Dunkirk days. It knows only one direction to take, and that is to sail on . . . and on . . . and on.

When we were last in Plymouth, we stood on the great green flat-topped hill they call the Hoe and re-visited the statue of Sir Francis Drake, who was bowling on the green there when the word came that the Spanish Armada was on its way to destroy England. It was from Plymouth Harbour that Drake then sailed to score one of the greatest naval victories in the history of the world. It was from this same harbor that Francis Chichester sailed in Gypsy Moth IV to circle the globe; and it was to that same quiet haven that he returned in triumph to be knighted by his Queen, who used the sword of Sir Francis Drake in the ceremony.

Oh, well—some people probably have little respect for a man who would be stupid enough to work his heart out at anything, much less the sport of sailing.

But there are still a few—one here, one there—a few in this prairie town, some more up that mountain hollow-whose hearts constrict when they read of Chichester's odysseys.

Masefield's poem furnished the title to Chichester's autobiography—the poem that begins:

"I must go down to the seas again,

To the lonely sea and the sky,

And all I ask is a tall ship

And a star to steer her by . . ."

So on these early autumn evenings when dusk falls and we glimpse the evening star riding high in the heavens, we may well wonder if Sir Francis isn't outward bound again, hull down for the Happy Isles.

The Longest Day

It is difficult to think that thirty whole years have come and gone since June 6, 1944.

In the late sixties we visited Torquay in southwest England, that roadstead where much of the invasion fleet made up, and from which they crossed the Channel. Torquay is a resort city, full of gay colors and distractions, and on the day we were there the wide harbor was aglitter with butter-gold sunlight that shimmered off the green water and enhanced the many-colored sails of the boats that were out in force.

Our mind flew back to that June day in 1944.

On that now-distant day we were at Princeton learning how to become a naval officer after being a seaman second-class. The winding walkways, the gracious lawns, the magnificent trees and the lovely ivy-clad buildings of the university were in sounding contrast to what was going on that day on the invasion beaches. Not until years later did we meet and talk with some of the paratroopers who had been part of the glider invasion the night before the invasion, whose craft had come slipping down out of the giddy darkness into the unknown fields of Normandy where so many never reached the ground alive.

A year or so ago we stood on the bluffs above the sea in Normandy. It was a perfect day in late September. The blue waters of the Channel washed gently up onto the beaches and lapped at the foot of the cliffs. These were the cliffs which the English troops and our Rangers had to scale in the face of devastating fire. On the top where we stood there were cows grazing around the ruins of the pillboxes which were now almost completely hidden by grass and bushes, and the smell of new-mown hay and honeysuckle was sweet and full of memories. A few miles to the south were the level beaches and gentle hills where the American infantry had stormed ashore. The landing beach there was all the deadlier because they were expected, and one can imagine the anguish and the chaos of that dim distant day. A short distance away on the higher ground is the American cemetery. It is meticulously kept with lovely green grass and lots of flowering shrubs stippled about among the clean white crosses. There is a quality that is indescribably haunting about the American flag that floats forever in the pale blue air at half mast. (Do flags still mean anything?)

Now, less than half the people alive in our America remember anything at all about that D-Day.

They have never experienced that spirit of resolution and dedication to something beyond one's self that motivated this nation to take its stand beside its English cousins and win the victory that had to be won to rescue Western civilization from Hitler's insane dream.

In a matter of months after D-Day, we were in the South Pacific. We were never involved in combat such as our military forces experienced in Normandy—it was our good fortune to escape such a holocaust.

Yet time after time as we stopped in the cloudy green islands we would visit the little cemeteries there. The words of James Michener come to mind:

"Before me lay the dead, the heroic dead who took the island. Upon a strange plateau, on a strange island, in a strange sea, far from their farms and villages, they slept forever beside the lagoon which bore them to their day of battle. Over them the sea birds dipped in endless homage. Above them the deep sky erected a cathedral."

At war's end, we were anchored off Biak Island.

June 6 was the anniversary of the turning point of that war, and so many of the sights and sounds and smells come back—yes, and the feelings.

One remembers the smell of the diesel exhaust from the myriad landing craft, and standing on the metal deck of an LCVP as it bobbed up and down in the heaving oily water. One remembers the air fields and the planes: the B-17's, the B-24's, the B-26's, and the huge B-29's . . . and the navy planes: The Hellcats, the Dauntlesses, the Corsairs, and the big lumbering PBY's. And one remembers the spindly, fleet-winged P-38's.

There are other sensory recollections:

The feel of the rain stinging the face as one clung to the blinker light, struggling to send and receive messages in a gale.

The cordite smell in the salt air after the guns spoke.

The living feel of the ship as it wallowed its way through the vast blue waters with the flying fish skimming just over the waves and a huge albatross gliding low and almost touching the wrinkled hilltops of water.

There are these and millions more, and they come flooding back on this anniversary.

But mostly, one is filled with a sense of wonder: Of wonder that men could rise to the heights, as they did at Dunkirk, at Iwo Jima, and perhaps most of all, on the Normandy beachheads.

136

As Sir Arthur Bryant so well put it, "everything comes to him who waits and, under God's providence, works hard enough for it."

But it takes—well, commitment is probably the right word.

General Montgomery, in his Order of the Day on D-Day, quoted Montrose's words:

"He either fears his fate too much, Or his deserts are small,

That dares not put it to the touch, To gain or lose it all."

And the most troubling wonder of all is that of whether we still have the kind of commitment that could make D-Day possible.

Time will tell.

Tall Ships Carry Tall Men

Ships don't always have to be tall of mast to be tall in other ways.

Indeed, the true tallness of ships depends upon the men who man them.

As beautiful as were the canvas-winged lovelies that graced New York's harbor on July 4, 1976, one could not but reflect on the tiny craft that Columbus navigated across the uncharted wilderness of alien waters, and the minute Mayflower, a ship so small as to be little more than a boat.

And what about Gypsy Moth IV and its indomitable one-man crew, Francis Chichester?

As further examples, we recall a couple of incidents from World War II:

'At Dunkirk, when the British army had been driven back, back to the sea, surrounded by Hitler's legions, and facing certain annihilation, a miracle occurred: from every cove, every harbor, every river mouth in England the little ships and boats began to pour forth across the Channel, usually so rough and turbulent, but on this day miraculously calm. They went to pick up and ferry home to safety the soldiers of their beleaguered army. Hundreds of thousands were borne across.

Those tiny ships were tall indeed!'

Again, after the United States had entered the war, an event occurred at Leyte Gulf in the Philippines in which the matter of size figured—or did not figure, depending upon how you look at it.

The American third Fleet had steamed north under Adm. "Bull" Halsey, leaving behind only a melange of lesser craft—some small carriers, destroyers and destroyer-escorts—when suddenly one day through the Straits of Surigao came the enormity of the Japanese fleet. Huge battleships—including the Yamamoto, with its 18-inch guns—heavy and light cruisers, destroyers, loomed up on the distant horizon. The situation was obviously hopeless.

Then it was that Adm. "Ziggy" Sprague, the commander of the American rag-tags, issued his famous order:

"Small boys make runs and make smoke."

And they did. Chattanooga's own, "Hobby" Law was there as gunnery officer of the Fanshaw Bay.

Straight toward the Goliaths that were bearing down on them the little Davids headed . . . and then . . . and then, for reasons never fully understood, the Japanese fleet fired briefly and terribly, turned, retreated over the horizon, and was gone!

It is good that on the Fourth of July we should think of ships that have stood tall in the history of our nation.

Yet amongst the tallest are a trio that we cannot altogether claim as our own:

It was dusk in Tel Aviv on July 3, 1976, when three American-made planes, ships of the air that, like the Yankee Clippers, ride the wings of the wind, lifted off the runways and streaked southward and west under the ever-brightening stars. It was just after midnight and early morning of July 4, when they coasted down to a smooth landing at the obscure Ugandan airport of Entebbe. There the Commandos piled out, brushed aside all resistance, stormed into an airport building, rescued the more than 100 hostages held there, and then reboarded their ships for a swift return to their homeland.

What a bold and imaginative feat!

How incredibly inspiring!

And how few are the nations today that have the raw courage to do what has to be done!

We hope it will never be forgotten that this daring rescue was on our own July 4 . . . a day of pride and courage.

The morning of July 5 dawned with the rains gone and a slender bit of sun slanting down across the wet green lawn to touch the brown trunks of the pine trees that stood so quiet and so tall.

As we bore the flag out to reset it in its socket on the side of the house wall, we thought once more how material tallness does not necessarily equate with moral tallness.

The early sunlight touched the Stars and the Stripes with its pale gold fingers, and our eyes picked out one of the white stars. Gazing at it, so sun-splashed and proud, we found our thoughts turning back to just over a month ago when we re-visited the lovely green-swarded American cemetery high on the cliffs above the Normandy invasion beaches. In that quiet and now peaceful place the music of the sea below is but dimly heard in the background and the gulls wheel and glide in the blue air. Dotted among the rows of snowy marble crosses one sees here and there the white Stars of David that mark the resting place of the Jewish boys.

How proud they would be of those rescue riders of the night wind, whose ships were tall, indeed!

An Answer in the Schools?

The little boy left his mother and entered the classroom. It was full of strangers, and there were the strange smells of the oiled floor, the chalk, the paste, and the rubbery smell of the cloakroom. His heart was filled with a mixture of fear and excitement and joy. What were the words he had heard? . . .

"Reading and 'riting and 'rithmetic
Taught to the tune of a hickory stick . . ."
This is the way it was.

Today it's different.

Harsh and dramatic changes have occurred in our public schools. There is a sharp decline in morale and in learning. News articles and editorials note much lower SAT scores and a worsening climate of the classroom where ignorance, violence and insubordination are often rampant.

Even worse are the values being acquired (or not acquired). A society is shaped by its values.

What is the reason?

We have been misguided by the social engineers who decided that everyone was equal, and that the way to Utopia was to forcibly mix students of different abilities and backgrounds and races—the illiterates with the literates, the unmannerly with the mannerly, the educable with the uneducable. Certain individuals can be trained, but cannot be educated.

Our Supreme Court was quite right when it held that no one should be denied opportunity because of race. But it was quite wrong when it equated desegregation with forced integration—opportunity with a quota system.

If you mix good and bad, the good is damaged more than the bad is helped.

And, lest this be thought racist, listen to the voices of some Responsible blacks—as contrasted with the Irresponsibles:

Wendell Gunn of Morristown, N.J., writing recently in the Wall Street Journal, says of the blacks' struggle:

"Our fight has not been, as some seem to think, for an immediate and equal share in America's wealth, but rather for equal access to America's promise—i.e., the opportunity to contribute to society and, in turn, reap benefits commensurate with those contributions." (Good.)

He adds:

"However, to extend the guarantee of equality beyond that goes directly against human nature . . . Individuals in a free society strive to produce above the average because of the prospect of reaping benefits which are also above the average." (Better.)

And then:

"In other words, individuals . . . specifically strive toward **inequality**. (Emphasis added) To promise equality of reward regardless of contribution . . . is to destroy the prime incentive of the potentially productive." (Best!)

Black columnist Lee May of the Atlanta Constitution, quotes a young teacher who recently decided to quit:

"To me, discipline is the major problem. If I could have gotten out of each class all the discipline problems, that may have left 10 to 15 students or it may have left five. But I could have taught those students if I didn't have the hecklers . . . Maybe when education turns around and gets itself straightened back out, I could go back . . ."

The solution?

Let students go to the school of their choice, so long as they live up to its standards as to grades and conduct.

Stop forcing competent students and incompetent students together. Use a "tracking system" in which students are put with others of relatively comparable ability, so they have a chance to compete and respond to challenge.

Enforce discipline. Expel those students who don't accept it.

Ask Claude Bond what he and his teachers at Howard High did 25 years ago when they had discipline problems. Why not now?

If City High could be run on a basis of good grades and discipline, what a different story it would be! Ask the teachers.

If scientists discovered a new virus they thought beneficial, but which turned out to be deadly, would they obstinately go on feeding, developing and proliferating it? That's what's being done with our schools.

As we taste the bitter fruit of the past two score years, we should heed the wry wisdom of the late Justice Brandeis who wrote:

"The greatest danger to liberty lies in the insidious encroachment by men of zeal, well-meaning, but without understanding."

It's not enough to wring our hands and hope for things to get better. Admit what is wrong and do something about it.

141

Isn't there someone somewhere who will investigate and report on what's what? Springer Gibson did it about five years ago in a series covering Dr. Colbert Whitaker's doctoral thesis.

It could make all the difference!

Requiem to a Storyteller

It has been several months since I learned that the Storyteller was dead. Now, belatedly, I want to say something about it.

There it was on the front page of the newspaper, plain as black and white.

"Well,"—you might say—"so what? Everyone dies, sooner or later. Even—believe it or not!—yourself."

Of course.

But it was so sudden, so unexpected, and the family and the friends (and the children) must have been terrible upset.

"The children?" say you, quizzically—"Aren't they part of 'the family'? Aren't you being redundant?"

No.

The children of whom I speak are all those children who have read and loved, and still read and love, and will read and love, Billy Steele's stories, books, tales of adventure.

For Billy Steele was a storyteller.

Storytelling is an ancient and honorable art, stretching all the way back to blind Homer and even beyond, and includes such as Virgil, Boccaccio, R.L. Stevenson, Jeffrey Farnol, Arthur Conan Doyle, and Saki, to mention but a few.

Billy Steele wrote many of the signs that mark the trails and roads in Reflection Riding at the request of his friend, my father, and whenever I see them, I hear him speaking to me.

"Words alone are certain good . . ."

So wrote W.B. Yeats, in my opinion the greatest of our twentieth century lyric poets.

At a time when words are becoming less thoughtfully read, less well written, and less truly understood, it is indeed tragic that one of our gifted wordsmiths should be so abruptly snatched away by Death, the Proud Brother.

His becoming a part of the Govan Clan was fit and proper for the Storyteller. That clan has always stood for the best in words and letters, as a host of word-people would testify.

Some years ago Nan Fairbrother, the lovely and gifted English author of "Men and Gardens" and other equally delightful books, visited Chattanooga and she especially enjoyed Billy and his wife Mary Steele and their family.

Once upon a time I discovered a poem by John Holmes that says how many of us feel about storytellers and those who read aloud:

"The voice, the voice burns on like flame.
            A listener looks through, to the back of his mind,
Past red-gold slope and spire of words looking.
            You read aloud to the ill, the young, the blind.
You read to the hundred faces with no name,
            Or to the beloved, the proudest words you find.
They forget you the first word out of your mouth.
            Not to be remembered for speaking loud or low,
But that a story lives its little space in time,
            So real the rain is wet, and they hear horses go—.
What a good way to be forgotten, into a story,
            A remembered sound of words when self is gone,
As a fire unburned, wood back to the woodpile,
            Or word returned to the shelf it stood upon.

To be taken down again, opened again, burned again,
            The book as your voice knowing its immortal power.
Reading aloud you raise up the golden wall
            Where the gold bough in the holy city sings an hour
Of glory, a poem of the honor and grief of men—
            And the speaker of poems remembered not at all."

Can't you just see that special corner of the great Hall in the Celestial City where all the children, young and old, who love stories, are gathered around the Storyteller to hear his voice and enjoy his tales?

Outside, the November leaves rain down, cut loose by the silver sickle of the frost, but indoors a wood fire is blazing on the hearth, the flame-fairies dancing, red, blue, orange, the smell of woodsmoke as sweetly tantalizing as the Storyteller's story.

Yes—to paraphrase our poem—"what a good way to be remembered—into a story!!"

144

The Sweetest Music this Side of Heaven

This time of year is for remembering.

People, like leaves, go home again to the earth and the sky. Last year, Bing Crosby . . . Guy Lombardo . . . and so many more; in the past few days, Gene Tunney . . . Norman Rockwell . . . Dr. Fowle . . . Bill Keese . . . Mac Moore . . . Miss Margaret Orrell . . .

The memories flow.

It was late October in the sleepy little Middle Tennessee town of Lebanon. The waning sunlight was dusty, the brightly colored leaves were beginning to fall and already the air had the premonitory chill and sherry flavor of November.

A young law student sat in a tiny cluttered one-man barbershop just off the square on Main Street getting a haircut. The radio was on and suddenly there was a voice and a song he had never heard before, but would never forget. The voice was effortless, creamy-smooth, gentle and warm as spring sunlight, and it sang "Where the blue of the night . . . meets the gold of the day . . . someone . . .waits for . . . me."

So it was that in 1931 Bing Crosby entered my life . . . the same Bing who, years later sang "I'm dreaming of a white Christmas . . . just like the ones I used to know . . ."

the same Bing who, after playing a round of golf in Spain last fall dropped dead of a heart attack as he was walking toward the clubhouse.

In those dim distant days of the 30's, there were the Amos and Andy shows, the original Mills Brothers, and the unforgettable sounds of the Big Bands. One of them was Jan Garber's. A sweetness, a lilt, and a romantic dreaminess in his music once heard, stuck like a fish-hook in the heart and could not be dislodged.

But the biggest name of all for me—bigger than Ben Bernie or Hal Kemp or Russ Columbo, or even the matchless Paul Whiteman—was Guy Lombardo and his Royal Canadians. (While at Southwestern in Memphis, I played tenor banjo for a couple of years in a tiny band we absurdly called the Royal Collegians!)

Even today I can close my eyes and the Lombardo music comes flowing back: Charmaine, Avalon, Sweethearts on Parade, Everywhere

You Go, In Your Easter Bonnet, Coquette, and, always at the fade-out, Auld Lang Syne.

"The Sweetest Music This Side of Heaven" they called it. It was a good description.

Whatever happened to our music makers? Can't we find a few people who will give us more singable songs that tell us of beauty, and love, and joy, instead of horrid wrenching sounds that screech and batter and whine of the sour and the betrayed and the disillusioned?

Who was it that said "Let me write the songs of a nation, and I will tell you which way it will go?"

Where are we going? Where?

Are there no Gershwins, no Irving Berlins, no Cole Porters? Not even a Hank Williams, whose "Your Cheating Heart Will Tell on You" wrung response from millions of those hearts?

Thank heavens we still have a Wayne King to weave his magic spell! "The Waltz You Saved for Me" has been his theme song since he was playing in Chicago, far away and long ago. (Was it at the Aragon—or the Trianon?)

Late last fall Guy Lombardo, too, finished his terrestrial stand and moved on, and our hearts are pricked by the thorn of memory.

Several years ago he and his Royal Canadians came to the Tivoli. We sat in the semi-darkness before the program started, remembering how, half a century earlier, we had seen that splendid theater make its debut. Then the Royal Canadians began to play, and we were swept away by the cool woodwinds, the sharp brasses, and the rhythm, into what Yeats might have called "a dreamy, quiet delight."

One of the newer songs played that night was "To Dream the Impossible Dream" from "Man of La Mancha." And then, sure enough, as the end of the concert was reached, they swung into "Auld Lang Syne."

Pictorial sensory impressions flashed across the screen of the mind: a fraternity dance, and the perfumed scent of a girl's hair, Christmas of 1944, the day before leaving on a long journey to the war in the South Pacific, New Year's Eve 1945, in Times Square, the war over, and a brave New World ahead.

And so . . . ?

Well, somewhere over the rainbow and beyond the icy clutch of winter and mortality is a place where one will enjoy the Master Music of the ages. For each of us that Concert in the Sky will be different: for some it will be chamber music, for others, symphony—for some, opera, or maybe blue-grass, or the reedy ballads of wandering minstrels.

But for lots of us—some older, some younger—it will be music like

Bing's, or what we've always known and loved as the "Sweetest Music This Side of Heaven"—and will end with

"We'll tak a cup o' kindness yet
For auld lang syne."

For the Ending is also the Beginning, whether it be the New Year or the New Dimension into which we step when we join the leaves.

Friendships, Golden and Lasting

"With rue my heart is laden
for golden friends I had . . ."
. . . A.E. Housman

C.S. Lewis said of friendship that it "arises out of mere Companionship when two or more of the companions discover that they have in common some insight or even taste which the others do not share and which, till that moment, each believed to be his own unique treasure (or burden). The typical expression of opening Friendship would be something like, What? You too? I thought I was the only one!"

And, when we think of golden friends we've had, we are minded of the Charles McD. Puckettes.

Charlie and Elizabeth Gettys Puckette moved to Chattanooga nearly four decades ago and were our Neighbors Non-Pareil from the start.

He was general manager of *The Times*—a clear-thinking, articulate, strong and well-mannered gentleman, while she was an artistic, lovable, gracious and kind lady. Both were blessed with a twinkling sense of humor that was never acid or sarcastic and was directed most frequently towards themselves.

Although in their early married life they had lived in Ridgewood, N.J., while Charlie worked in New York City, they were both native Tennesseans—he from Sewanee, and she from Ingleside, the Gettys family place, near Athens. They met in New York where he was working for the old *New York Evening Post* and she was studying art at the Art Students League. Both of them roomed at Miss Yorsten's Home for Genteel Southern Ladies and Gentlemen and she loved to tell the story of how they were the only two boarders there who breakfasted early in the dining room, and how, one morning, Charlie—reserved and dignified as always—was having breakfast across the table from her when, lowering the paper he was reading, he addressed her to ask if she would marry him.

She did.

Her recent death was on the anniversary of his burial, 22 years before.

We well remember the day of his funeral, one of those harsh cold January days that remind one of Auden's poem "In Memory of W.B. Yeats" which said:
"What instruments we have agree
The day of his death was a dark cold day."

Yet what we recall most vividly about that day was our reaction when the priest intoned the majestic words of the burial service as they appear in the 1928 Book of Common Prayer:

"I know that my Redeemer liveth, and that he shall stand at the latter day upon the earth: and though this body be destroyed, yet shall I see God: whom I shall see for myself, and mine eyes shall behold, and not as a stranger."

Charlie Puckette—loyal churchman, vestryman, senior warden, generous, honorable—would certainly behold God as no stranger.

And we are sure that the same was true of her, for whenever, wherever, and whatever, the need for Christian kindness, love, giving, she was there to give it.

Their children carry on the same tradition: Charlie, Isabelle, Stephen, and the grandchildren. All hold to the same high standards.

Though it be contrary to "el espiritu del tiempo" today, one is moved to say that they have good blood in them.

Indeed, it's of the best.

And just as we are convinced that with the turn of the year another spring will come, and the north-riding sun will sound its golden trumpet-call to wake the sleeping flowers, we're equally sure that there will come the time of Resurrection and Reunion of all those "golden friends we had."

Our beloved Joe Nichols, who conducted her funeral service, gave just the right touch with this prayer:

"We come to give her back to Thee, dear God, who gavest her to us. Yet as Thou didst not lose her in giving, so we have not lost her by her return. Not as the world giveth, givest Thou, O Lover of souls. What thou givest Thou takest not away. For what is Thine is ours, if we are Thine. Life is eternal and love is immortal and death is only a horizon, and a horizon is nothing save the limit of our sight.

"Lift us up, Strong Son of God, that we may see farther; cleanse our eyes that we may see more clearly; draw us closer to Thyself that we may know ourselves nearer to our beloved who are with Thee. And while Thou dost prepare a place for us, prepare us for that happy place, that where they are, and Thou art, we too may be."

It was one of her favorite prayers.

And it explains why we could re-write Housman's poem to read:
"With thanks our hearts are laden
for golden friends we've had . . ."
For they are!

Thumbs and Gardens

According to Nan Fairbrother, an old Chinese proverb says that "If you would be happy for a week, take a wife: If you would be happy for a month, kill your pig: If you would be happy all your life, plant a garden."

Tuesday, January 8, 1980, marked the Diamond Wedding Anniversary of a couple who have succeeded in the pursuit of a happy significance.

Mr. and Mrs. Thumb, as I will call them, have proven—and disproven— the validity of the proverb: they have been both (happily) married and gardening for a lifetime.

As to the pig—I just don't know.

Born over eight decades ago in Elgin, Ill., Mr. T. studied horticulture at the University of Illinois, In 1915 he moved with his parents to Chattanooga, where his father managed the Southern Skein and Foundry plant in East Lake.

When America entered World War I, young Thumb enlisted in Cavalry Troop B, commanded by Major Fyffe and Captain Doug McMillin, was sent to Greenville, South Carolina, for training and then overseas, where he was transferred to the 114th Machine Gun outfit.

There he suddenly found himself converted—into a handler of carrier pigeons.

It's hard for us today to realize how important those fleet-winged birds were in that pre-radio war. For example: in a particularly bloody battle, an American unit got trapped and surrounded by Germans. Cut off for days, they were out of food and ammunition . . . they had two boxes of Mr. T.'s pigeons, twenty-four to the box, but they had eaten all but four when they decided to try to get a message though. One lone pigeon, battered, terrified and exhausted, made it with its coded message, and within two hours American planes were dropping food and ammunition to the beleaguered outfit, which fought its way out of the trap. And Mr. T.'s heroic pigeon was gratefully named "Bon Ami"— Good Friend!

When the war ended, Sgt. T. was honorably discharged, and then returned to Illinois and succeeded in getting his boyhood sweetheart, Ruth, to marry him. . .

Robert Sparks Walker's friendly assistance and the kind intervention of Frank Nelson enabled young Mr. T. to come to Chattanooga with his bride and to go immediately into the work he has always enjoyed most— landscape gardening. And quickly he and those for whom he worked discovered that he possessed almost miraculous ability to understand and even communicate with plants, trees, shrubs and flowers.

Some outstanding examples of his genius included plantings at the Bright School, Dixie Yarns, the Coca-Cola Company and Happy Valley farms, as well as at such homes as those of C.D. Little, Peyton Carter, Summerfield Johnston and the Ed Coopers . . .

Among other clients who were also good friends were Don and Ruth Overmyer, the late Lavens Thomas, John Fowler, Carl Cartinhour, Frank Robbins—and there are many more.

To some he ascribed nicknames, such as "Hot-Shot," "Lord Plushbottom," "Buddy," and "The Oracle of Lookout Mountain." (All will remain unidentified.)

The T.'s have two daughters and four grandchildren, thus demonstrating that they are good at growing people as well as plants.

For more than half a century now, the Thumbs have lived on the sunset side of a hill overlooking the campus of Baylor School. From their home they can see the shining waters of the mighty Tennessee River as it flows majestically past Williams Island and enters the narrow gorge between Elder and Signal mountains.

Gardening imparts wisdom. One comes to recognize the truth of the 103rd Psalm which says, "As for man, his days are as grass: as a flower of the field, so he flourisheth. For the wind passeth over it and it is gone."

Gardening also teaches that we are but loaned the things of beauty that we possess, or think we possess . . . the season turns, the flower fades . . . but we know that already another blossom is forming.

Yet the best that anyone comes to know is that the most precious flower of all is that of friendship . . . a relationship of love uncomplicated by any sense of being bound.

Rudyard Kipling, whose wisdom and poetry have lately and unfortunately been neglected, once wrote a poem entitled "The Glory of the Garden." Part of it goes as follows:

"Our England is a garden, and such gardens are not made
By singing: 'Oh, how beautiful!' and sitting in the shade
While better men than we go out and start their working lives
At grubbing weeds from gravel paths with broken dinner knives.

There's not a pair of legs so thin, there's not a head so thick,
There's not a hand so weak and white, nor yet a heart so sick,
But it can find some needful job that's crying to be done,
For the Glory of the Garden glorifieth everyone.
Then seek your job with thankfulness and work till further orders,
If it's only netting strawberries or killing slugs on borders:
And when your back stops aching and your hands begin to harden,
You will find yourself a partner in the Glory of the Garden.
Oh, Adam was a gardener, and God who made him sees
That half a proper gardener's work is done upon his knees,
So when your work is finished you can wash your hands and pray
For the Glory of the Garden that it may not pass away!
And the Glory of the Garden it shall never pass away!"
These are the Thumb sentiments.

So, in this early January season, when all the flowers and trees and shrubs lie dormant, awaiting the golden trumpet call of yet another spring, we do well to honor a couple who might, indeed, have been named Mr. and Mrs. Green Thumb—but who are actually Mr. and Mrs. E. Kern Smith.

And may the Glory of the Garden never pass away!

The Icarus Complex

As I was flying from Philadelphia to Atlanta two years ago, I noticed a shield affixed to the forward bulkhead which bore the legend: "Celebrating 50 years: Delta Air Line— 1929-1979."

It reminded me that my own span of air travel was identical.

In June 1929, our father took me (age 18) and my next two younger brothers, along with a friend of his, to England. We went by sea, over on the Majestic and back on the Leviathan. It was my initiation into international travel, and the first of a series of odysseys that have continued half a century.

It was also my introduction to the intoxicating world of flight.

After a couple of sun-splashed weeks in southern England, we booked air passage to Paris. My two brothers and our father went on one plane, and Carl Cartinhour, my father's friend and I on another (for discretion's sake!)

We flew in a Ford Tri-Motor, sometimes irreverently called a "Tin Goose." Its body, encased in a sort of waffled sheet metal, shimmied and shook. It boasted one propeller-engine on its nose and one on each wing. Frightfully noisy, it lumbered clumsily skyward from Croyden (then nothing but a grassy meadow), and thundered away at low altitude over the green Sussex downs and the twinkling blue water of the English Channel to land, with a goose-like bump, at Le Bourget airport.

After ten days in the City of Light, where we put up at the Grand Hotel, we again took wing, returned to London, then went down by train to Southampton to take ship for home.

For nearly 40 years thereafter I never saw another Tin Goose. Then, one day as we wandered through the Deutsch Museum in Munich, lo! . . . there was one, hanging like a huge stuffed bird from the ceiling!

It's impossible to define the feel of flying—a delight to many, but a horror to some. Flight is at once so natural and yet so unnatural.

You recall the mythological story of Icarus and his father Daedelus: how the old man had learned to fly by using wings made of feathers. Then he made a second set and fastened one pair to his own shoulders and the other to those of his son. They worked perfectly. The father warned the lad to be careful not to fly too high lest the heat of the sun

154

melt the wax that stuck the feathers together. But Icarus, drunk on the heady wine of flight, ignored his father's warning and went on up, and up, and up—until suddenly the wax did melt, the wings came apart, and down, down he tumbled, spinning through the thinny air to fall int the blue waters of that sun-glittering sea which now bears his name.

During the half century since my own and Delta's first flights, much has changed.

Airships, rigid and semi-rigid, have come and gone.

The piston engine has been replaced by the jet (which transforms the airplane from a flying machine to a projectile)

Speed has increased from about 100 to over 500 m.p.h. on regular jets, 1,400 on the Concorde, and over 2,000 on some military jets.

From planes carrying a dozen passengers, we've come to the 747's, carrying 400 to 500.

Continents have been laced to within a few hours of each other, instead of days or weeks . . . or months.

On the grimmer side, we now have skyjackers, terrorists and the jubilant shooting down of innocent civilian passenger planes by savage and uncivilized people.

Recently, I came across a description of an earlier type of flight in the words of an English balloonist, who wrote it in 1927:

"I am alone in a very small balloon over Surrey on the last day of a beautiful May . . . Very slowly I approach a big wood . . .

"Fifteen hundred feet up, an almost absolute silence, broken occasionally by the barking of a dog heard very faintly, or by a voice hailing the balloon, and by an occasional friendly creak of the basket and rigging if I move ever so slightly. Then quite suddenly I am aware of something new.

"The balloon has come down a little already, and I scatter a few handfuls of sand and await the certain result. But my attention is no longer on that, it is arrested by this new sound which I hear, surely the most wonderful and sweetest sound heard by mortal ears. It is the combined singing of thousands of birds, of half the kinds which make the English spring so lovely. I do not hear one above the others; all are blended together in a wonderful harmony without change of pitch or tone, yet never wearying the ear."

That must be the sort of quiet ecstasy experienced by those who fly sail-planes, or even those Icarian follies, the hang-gliders.

My favorite flyers must include the remarkable Englishman, Francis Chichester; our quiet American, Charles Lindbergh; and the poetic

Frenchman Antoine St. Exupery, whose "Night Flight," "Wind, Sand and Stars" and "Flight From Arras" are gems of literature, as is his incomparable "The Little Prince."

But surely one of the most moving compositions by those who have ridden Pegasus across the swift, blue meadows of the upper air, is that penned during World War II by John Magee:

"Oh, I have slipped the surly bonds of earth,
And danced the skies on laughter-silvered wings;
Sunward I've climbed and joined the tumbling mirth
Of sun-split clouds—and done a hundred things
You have not dreamed of—wheeled and soared and swung
High in the sunlit silence. Hovering there,
I've chased the shouting wind along and flung
My eager craft through footless halls of air.
Up, up the long delirious, burning blue
I've topped the wind-swept heights with easy grace,
Where never lark, or even eagle, flew;
And, while with silent, lifting mind I've trod
The high untrespassed sanctity of space,
Put out my hand, and touched the face of God."

May all who share the Icarus complex feel the ecstasy—and always have Happy Landings!

For Liberty Ships

A recent news story told of the last of the nations's World War II
Liberty ships being quietly buried at sea.

These cargo vessels, built during World War II and mothballed after
the War's end, had become too great a problem of caretaking . . . so
they were towed away to be scuttled and sunk to form artificial reefs to
improve fishing grounds.

Something clicked, memories woke, and pictures . . . sounds . . .
feelings . . . flooded back.

An Armed Guard gun crew furnished the sole defense for the civil-
ian-manned cargo ships—most of which were Liberty ships—that carried war materiel and supplies around the world to the Army.

Because the Armed Guard were Navy and drew the scanty pay of
military personnel, the Merchant Marine tended to look down on them.
That is—until trouble came.

Then, well—you remember Kipling's poem "Tommy:"

"I went into a public-'ouse to get a pint o' beer,
The publican 'e up an' sez, 'We serve no red-coats here.'
The girls be'ind the bar they laughed an' giggled fit to die,
I outs into the street again an' to myself sez I:
'. . . It's Tommy this, an' Tommy that, an' 'Chuck him out, the
    brute!'
But it's 'Savior of 'is country' when the guns begin to shoot . . ."

It was a sun splashed day in New Orleans in the late fall of 1944,
when, a brand-new lieutenant (jg), I clambered aboard the SS R.M
Pearson, a typical Liberty ship of about ten thousand tons, to take
command of the Armed Guard crew. I was an ancient of thirty-four,
while most of them were in their low twenties or late teens.

One—stocky, blue-eyed, and from Chicago—strode up to me, grinned,
stuck out his hand and said, "Sir, I'm Ray Nicolci . . ." and he's been
part of me ever since.

Departing New Orleans, we crossed the Gulf of Mexico (getting our
first glimpse of flying fish) to Panama, traversed the Canal, and then,

for countless days, plodded westward and south, seeing nothing but blue sea and sky—"a painted ship upon a painted ocean."

Our first landfall was Manus Island in the Admiralties—and thence on to Hollandia, in New Guinea. From there we steamed north in convoy to the Gulf of Leyte in the Philippines. And, finally, ending up at Iloilo, the capital of Panay Island, we unloaded our cargo and glimpsed our first flame tree . . . the splendid "arbol de fuego."

The Pearson returned to the States—but only after I and several of my crew had been re-assigned to a smaller vessel of ancient decrepitude, whereon we served until the War's end.

A ship is a world in microcosm. You become a part of her, and learn to find your way about in total darkness. Like a steam locomotive, she is a creature alive—the throb of her engines, the creak of her joints, her wallowing and panting, all speak of her vitality.

And, like all living creatures, she requires interdependence—a submission to the will of others—the giving up of freedom and liberty . . . in order to obtain them.

Gun crews are at battle stations well before sunrise and sunset and remain there until broad daylight or total darkness. Twilight—whether morning or evening—is the favorite time for submarines to attack.

Memories:

"It was grey dawn when I woke. Within a minute and a half I was on the bridge—I was in no hurry . . .

"The sea was calm, glassy . . . The last stars were paling in the lightening air . . . On the rim of the world colors burned cool and fragile . . . The ships about us were like toys carved of ebony and set upon a green glass-topped table . . . They seemed scarcely to move . . .

And again:

"Night had risen like dark vapor from the face of the deep to fill the cooling air. Only a few clouds in the west still showed the last luminous colors of the buried sun, and in the east, Rigel, Capella, Aldebaran and bright Sirius had lit their tiny trembling lamps. The foam churned up by the blunt, thrusting prow of the plodding ship swept past below the wing of the flying bridge where the lieutenant leaned on the rail, gazing down at the carded white of the foam, and the fitful glow of the phosphorous came and went in the dark water like aquatic fireflies . . ."

On the wall of my office hangs a painting of a Liberty ship in convoy, with a heavy sea running. It looks to be in the North Atlantic, where the ferocity of the sub packs and the bitter cold of the water made the job almost suicidal.

I look at her and I remember.

I remember the fear—and, afterwards, the enormous relief.

And I remember the friends I had who did not come back.

They, like these ships, have gone down to the sea . . . forever . . . and I breathe a silent prayer: "Requiescant in pace!"

And is it only the worn-out bodies of the ships that are gone—and not the Liberty itself?

Pray God it is!

D-Day— 40 Years Ago

Forty years ago this June 6 an event took place that altered the course of history: the invasion of Fortress Europe by the Allied Forces—the most massive, daring and well-executed military maneuver in recorded history.

Following WWI, in which Kaiser Wilhelm's Germany sought to conquer Western Europe and failed, there was a decade of peace, during which Germany suffered depression and bankruptcy. Then an Austrian house painter named Adolph Hitler began to kindle the spirit of nationalism in Germany. He was so successful that in 1939 they launched a blitzkrieg effort to do what they'd tried unsuccessfully before. Their initial conquest was that of Poland . . . but England—good old solid, stolid England, having pledged to support Poland if invaded, went to war with the Nazis, as did France.

A year or so of stalemate followed . . . Then the Germans unleashed an all-out attack, sweeping around the end of the vaunted Maginot Line and driving the French and British forces back to the English Channel. At Dunkirk, the remnants of the British Army were saved only by the grace of God and the thousands of small craft that ferried back and forth across the miraculously calm waters of the Channel to bring home the exhausted soldiers stranded on the beaches . . .(Have you read Paul Gallico's *The Snow Goose?*).

It was at that critical time, as England awaited invasion of their island, that something happened. Sir Arthur Bryant, England's greatest living historian, puts it thusly:

"The voice that came out of England at that moment was neither repentant nor submissive . . . it was the voice of a man angry, defiant and utterly resolved; or rather of 47-millions looking in a single direction, and that direction seawards, and intoning in their hearts the words which one of them spoke for all: 'We shall defend our island whatever the cost may be. We shall fight on the beaches; we shall fight on the landing-grounds; we shall fight in the fields and in the streets; we shall fight in the hills; and we shall never surrender.'"

As Churchill spoke, the spirit of all England responded.

Spitfires swarmed up out of the misty green meadows into the skies to defy the German bombers and fighters . . . Hitler hesitated, postponed his invasion . . . and the tide began to turn.

The following December, Japan, Hitler's ally in the Orient, made a sneak-attack on Pearl Harbor, and the United States entered the war.

No one who experienced that war, whether in the service or not, can never forget the spirit of common purpose that marked it. Names come floating back, bringing vivid pictures: Murmansk, Casablanca, Anzio, Guadalcanal, Midway, Leyte Gulf . . . The names ring like bells in the cloisters of memory.

June 6, 1944, was the Day of Decision.

For months the Allied Forces under Eisenhower had been planning an invasion that could lead to Hitler's defeat. A huge armada had been assembled. Troops were readied, aircraft prepared.

Unfortunately, the weather on the English Channel was so bad that it threatened disaster to the ships, the amphibious landings, and the aircraft.

Still, a decision must be made . . . and Eisenhower made it.

On June 6 the assault began, with the massive invasion of Normandy.

Anyone who visits the beaches of Normandy must wonder how it ever succeeded!

The English had to scale towering cliffs, climbing like spiders up ropes attached to grappling hooks shot up from below to snag in the grass at the top.

The Americans came in on the level beaches where the pillboxes and the massed Germans were waiting to slaughter them. Yet the landing craft kept coming in, the soldiers kept struggling ashore through the surf torn by the German guns, the paratroopers and gliders landed behind the German lines. The Allied planes bombed and strafed . . . and the invaders moved inland, and on to ultimate victory.

Not until recently did we learn how Eisenhower, waiting as his troops fought their way ashore, had prepared a hand-written memo to be released in the event the invasion had failed, in which he assumed full responsibility.

"Our landings . . . have failed to gain a satisfactory foothold and I have withdrawn the troops . . . My decision to attack . . . was based on the base information available. The troops, the Air and the Navy, did all that bravery and devotion to duty could do. If any blame or fault attached to the attempt, it is mine alone . . ."

Today, the scene on that Normandy coast is one of pastoral tranquility. The hedgerows are thick and green. Cows graze placidly in meadows dotted with flowers and sweet with the fragrance of honeysuckle and mown grass. Far below the lofty cliffs the azure sea is calm and peaceful, sunlight glinting off the water.

In the blue sky above the American Cemetery, white-winged gulls wheel and dip and float in the thin sparkling air. The white crosses and the Stars of David stand mutely at attention on the green grassy sward for as far as the eye can reach.

One glimpses the red, white and blue of the star-spangled flag at half-mast, forever grieving, and the tears come, unbidden.

Eisenhower and Winston Churchill were the Decision-Makers of Destiny.

They turned the shadow of death into morning. They sparked the effort that saved our western civilization, with the aid of those who served with them, including those who sleep in peace in the graves of Normandy and across the world . . .

"Lord God of Hosts, be with us yet—lest we forget, lest we forget!"

In Memory of Robert Nathan

It was Memorial Day, 1985, and the eastern sky was rosy with dawn. A wandering breeze stirred the rippling folds of the flag just outside the front door as I ventured out to pick up the paper, and I recalled standing on the green turf of the American cemetery on the coast of Normandy, moved by the beauty of the great flag that hung there at half-staff, grieving for the thousands whose graves are marked by the white marble crosses and the Stars of David. I remembered, too, the way the sunlight reflected off the blue-green waters of the sea, far below the steep cliffs, and the gulls soaring in the gusty wind, wings white against the sky.

As I re-entered the house and opened the paper, I was suddenly jolted in a different direction: "Robert Nathan dies" read the headline. Death, the proud brother of sleep, had taken one of my heroes.

More than a half century ago, Mr. Books (Gilbert Govan) who tended the bookstore at Paynes's, brought Nathan's writings into my life. It was love at first reading. In my early 20s then, I was deeply moved by a sonnet Gilbert quoted to me:

"I ride the great black horses of my heart
with reins of steel across their flying hair;
so slow are they to halt, so swift to start,
the stormy-breasted stallions of despair . . ."

The first of Nathan's brief, yet poignant, novels I read was *Jonah,* a tale about the Old Testament prophet. It contains the following passage:

"As evening fell, he found himself beside a little pool in the desert; here he sat down to rest. The sky was green with early night; the evening star, smaller than the moon and silver as a distant sea, sailed above Sharon. Before him lay the desert, heavy with silence, drenched with the cold dew of evening; Jonah shivered and drew his cloak about him.

"As he sat there, his head bowed upon his hands, a fox came out of a hole, and seeing Jonah, exclaimed: "There is the man of God.""

A spell was cast over me that has lasted ever since.

Among his many books are *Portrait of Jennie, One More Spring, Winter in April, The Bishop's Wife* and *The River Journey*—all quiet but powerfully moving masterpieces in miniature.

Yet, memorable as are his novels, his poems are even more so. Today not many know them, I suppose. Unfortunately, this may be one of those temporary Dark Ages that afflict affluent societies, when real poetry and music almost perish.

Even today, though, most would surely appreciate the haunting beauty of such lines as:

"Tread softly, sorrow, for the summer passes,

Her leaves are falling in continual rain;

Let me be silent as the withered grasses,

Let me be quiet as the gathered grain . . ."

or the equally nostalgic

"Now blue October, smoky is the sun,

Must end the long, sweet summer of the heart.

The last brief visit of the birds is done;

They sing the autumn songs before they part . . ."

Like Edna St. Vincent Millay, Nathan understood that real poetry is the love-child of music and painting. His own always combine pleasant and musical sounds with lovely color and flowing, graceful line. And there is profound wisdom in:

"Ask not for freedom if you fear to weep,

Or dream of peace if terror makes you start . . ."

Born in New York City in 1894, Robert Nathan was educated at Phillips Academy at Exeter, then at Harvard, where he was an editor of *The Harvard Monthly,* in which his first stories and poems appeared. Later, while working in an advertising agency in 1919, he published his first novel, *Peter Kindred,* which was followed by scores of others and by his poems. He quickly acquired a reputation as a master of satiric fantasy unique in American literature. An accomplished musical amateur, he was a skillful fencer, and was fond of swimming and tennis.

In mid-life he moved to the West Coast where he lived with his English-born wife, Anna, to whom he dedicated his last book of poems, *Evening Song.*

Because he and Mrs. Books (Christine Noble Govan) were such good friends, I always felt that somehow he was my friend, too. How fitting and proper that both should enter Valhalla this year!

Jack Smith, of the *Los Angeles Times,* relates that he had once written about the melancholy of Sunday afternoon and that Nathan had responded:

"Even children feel a vague sadness late of a Sunday afternoon, in that hour when the light has turned gray and cold and before the yellow lights are lit in the blue evening air. It is because Sunday is a special day, unlike any other . . .

"On Sunday, anything can happen, something marvelous . . . One waits for it all week; and then, as the day passes, and the light begins to fall, one realizes that nothing marvelous has happened at all.

"Old people feel like that, too. They look ahead to Sunday . . . only to realize, when it comes, that nothing marvelous has happened, or ever will; they are simply one week older. But there is this difference: by the time the lamps are lit, old people are already looking ahead to Monday when the world picks up again. Perhaps . . . on Monday . . . something marvelous . . ."

But most precious of all to me is his sonnet that tells so briefly, but truly, what lies in the heart of each of us:

"The heart in wonder, like a lonely wren,
Will sing a while and then be still as long.
He waits an answer ere he sings again,
Who sings for love, and not alone for song.
The birds's shy pipe will falter in the end,
The heart's voice sicken if it be not heard;
They seek the absent, the beloved friend—
Song is for lovers, whether heart or bird.
So, if you hear me, tell me that you hear,
Lest I grow weary and forget to sing;
As in this sweet green season of the year
The bird that hears no answer lifts his wing
And far away, dejected and remote,
Tried other woodlands with his lonely note."
Can you imagine leaving a better memorial?

Restore the Spirit of Liberty

July has come, a month of blazing heat, of sweat, and sometimes, of grateful, rain-sweet coolness. After the sun has set, shadows rise like blue mist from the hollows of the earth, and you hear the chorus of locusts, and smell the scent of mown grass.

In a long-ago childhood, it was a time of vegetables fresh from our garden: onions, and corn, and okra and tomatoes; of juicy, sweet peaches, and of watermelons, red-fleshed, crisp and cool after being chilled in spring water; and—oh, blessed taste!—of ice-cold lemonade, and of ice cream, hand-churned in the ice cream freezer (with coarse salt in with the ice). Sometimes you got to lick the dasher. It was also the time of June bugs, whose tiny lamps flickered in the shadowy darkness.

And there were fireworks. The Fourth was the centerpiece. There was a poem that fitted that day that began:
"Hats off! Along the street there comes
A blare of bugles, a ruffle of drums,
A flash of color beneath the sky:
Hats off! The flag is passing by!
Blue and crimson and white it shines
Over the steel-tipped, ordered lines.
Hats off! The colors before us fly;
But more than the flag is passing by . . ."

There were parades, and speeches, and picnics. Flags were flown, and the crowds that lined the street to watch the parade go by held tiny flags that they waved in time with such thumpety-thump music as Sousa's *Stars and Stripes Forever.*

Patriotism flowered.

What about July 4, 1986? It still stands, you know, for the spirit of independence, of freedom, of liberty, and (this year) the 100th birthday of the Statue of Liberty.

Perhaps we should read again the opening lines of Robert Nathan's *A Note to Politicians*:
"Gentlemen, let me remind you that liberty is not lost by revolution,
By the sudden appearance of armed men, the parade of tanks, machine guns drumming,

And the little flowers of men's regard, made out of steel and dyna
    mite,
Blossoming in the streets. All that comes later,
Or not at all. We can do without it. Gentlemen,
It is something else that weakens the freedom in us:
A worm in the wood, a little flaw in the flute;
It is this: that we are not sure that we want it.
It is this: that we give it away like bits of an old house,
For something new, a car, or a peck of potatoes . . .
Liberty, yours and mine, is lost by barter
Before we even begin to know we have lost it . . ."

Today, on July 4, 1986, we bask in the sentimental warmth of thoughts of "independence," "freedom," and "liberty."

What do the words really mean? "Independence" means relying on one's self. Today, alas, almost all of us are dependent on others.

A frightening number of Americans look entirely to the government to provide everything. Without realizing it, they have sold themselves into an insidious and tragic slavery. The closest any of us can come to true independence is to depend on dependable people—in other words, to live in dependence on those who are dependable.

What does "freedom" mean?

Obviously, it does not mean doing whatever one wishes. There is no absolute freedom. No one, whether CEO or editor or garbageman is really free to say what he thinks, since he may offend someone who can hurt him. And many so-called "freedom fighters" are, in reality, just terrorists.

And, finally, what about the word "liberty?"

In July 1944, while in the Navy, I wrote something that my friend Alfred Mynders put in a column in *The Times,* quoting from a speech by Judge Learned Hand, one of the greatest federal judges ever to grace the bench. The words had the simplicity, the earthy plainness and honesty of Lincoln's little talk at Gettysburg. They had the awe and humility and devotion of a man who is great, and who is better-than-average acquainted with God.

Of liberty, he said:

" . . . Liberty lies in the hearts of men and women; when it dies there, no Constitution, no law, no court can save it; no Constitution, no law, no court can even do much to help it. . . . The spirit of liberty is the spirit that is not too sure that it is right; the spirit of liberty is the spirit which seeks to understand the minds of other men and women; the spirit of liberty is the spirit which weighs their interests alongside its own without bias; the spirit of liberty remembers that not even a sparrow falls to earth unheeded; the spirit of liberty is the spirit of Him, who, near two thousand years ago, taught mankind a lesson it has never learned but never quite forgotten: that there may be a kingdom where the least shall be heard and considered side by side with the greatest . . ."

RANDOM CHOICE

Other Men's Flowers

December has come, bearing the silver needles of frost and the chill scent of mortality.

We remember Shakespeare's sonnet that begins:

"That time of year thou mayst in me behold/When yellow leaves, or none, or few, do hang./Upon these boughs that shake against the cold,/ Bare, ruined choirs, where late the sweet birds sang . . ."

And we remember, too, a funeral we attended last March.

The early spring sky was blue as a robin's egg, the trees on tip-toe, ready to burst into bloom. From somewhere came the tumbling, mercurial song of a mockingbird.

Pale golden sunlight bathed the slope of the National Cemetery hill where the greening earth was misty with tiny flowers. Beneath a tiny tent, a coffin lay quiet, covered by the proud white stars and scarlet stripes of the American flag. In and around the tent were those who had come for a final moment with a friend, unique and uniquely loved.

It was the funeral of E. Kern Smith, sometimes known as Mr. Green Thumb.

The Rev. Arnold Slater spoke first. Those present, he said, had come to share their sense of loss and of love for a man who had been "a working partner with God." A landscape architect, he observed, was one "who has the vision, plants the seed, and then God produces the results."

And now, he went on, our friend who had slipped away quietly during his sleep, was to spend an aeon or two tending God's own garden.

"I will lift up mine eyes unto the hills," he read—and everyone could see Kern standing, sturdy and strong even in his 80s, on his flower-flooded hillside above Baylor School, looking clear-eyed down the canyon of the Tennessee River to the beckoning swell of the mountains beyond.

As the Rev. Slater went on to say, Kern was a man who could be gruff, even testy, with those who evidenced stupidity, but he was possessed of a rich sense of humor. The only thing he enjoyed more than hearing a good story was telling one.

170

Then he spoke of Ruth, Kern's ever-present and always helpful wife, who moved here with her young husband three score years ago, soon after World War I.

In that war, Kern had had charge of his unit's carrier pigeons—there were no radios then—and one of his pigeons, the famous Bon Ami, successfully zig-zagged through shot and shell to summon rescue to an entrapped American outfit. "Good Friend" indeed!

Finally, the Rev. David Beebe read selections from scripture, and quoted the most beautiful of all prayers from the Book of Common Prayer:

"O Lord support us all the day
long
until the shadows lengthen and the
evening comes and the busy world
is hushed, and the fever of life is
over, and our work is done. Then,
in
thy mercy, grant us a safe lodging
and a holy rest, and peace at last."

The funeral was over.

Afterward, one of Kern's closest friends, whom he always called "Honest Martha," quoted a poem as we stood looking out over the headstones, remembering Chateau Thierry, Verdun, and the marble crosses in the American cemetery, high above the Normandy beachhead, where the gulls' curving flight is scribed upon the flag-blue air:

"In Flanders fields the poppies
blow
Between the crosses, row on row
That mark our place; and in the
sky
The larks, still bravely singing, fly,
Scarce heard amid the guns below.
We are the dead. Short days ago
We lived, felt dawn, saw sunset
flow,
Loved and were loved . . .and now
we lie
In Flanders' field . . ."

And again, as we walked slowly away and back to our respective car, she recited Stevenson's immortal "Requiem"":

"Under the wide and starry sky,
Dig the grave and let me lie;

171

Glad did I live, and gladly die,
And I laid me down with a will . . .
This be the verse you grave for me:
Here he lies where he long'd to be;
Home is the sailor, from sea,
And the hunter home from the
hill."

Both quotations are in Viscount Archibald Wavell's personal anthology of poems called "Other Men's Flowers." In that book's preface, Wavell, one of England's heroes in the Middle East in World War II, quoted Montaigne:

"I have gathered a posie of other men's flowers,/and nothing but the thread that binds them is my own."

So in a sense, it was with our landscape architect, our gardener, our friend, E. Kern Smith.

The trees, the landscapes, the flowers he touched, tended and loved, were for the most part, those of other men.

Yet—were they really?

Does any of us really own anything?

Last of the Line

On the front page of the *Times* appeared the following story:

Nairobi, Kenya Dec. 25 (AP)—Maj. Earl Wavell, 37, son of the late Field Marshal Wavell, was killed by Mau Mau terrorists last night.

He was leading a Black Watch patrol investigating the beheading of an African loyal to the British when his patrol was ambushed by the Mau Mau, an organization whose members have sworn to drive the white man out of Kenya. Wavell fell early in the encounter.

In the early days of WW2, Rommel, the Desert Fox, was held at bay in North Africa by a tiny British army under the brilliant and courageous leadership of Field Marshall A.P. Wavell. So daring and so effective was the military genius of the one-eyes soldier that he was made a viscount, and his name is high on the rolls of England's heroes.

Since then, both Viscount Wavell and his foe Rommel have died.

In 1945, just after the close of World War II, Viscount Wavell published a book. It was called "Other Men's Flowers" and was sub-titled "An Anthology of Poems Compiled by A.P. Wavell." The title came from Montaigne, who once wrote: "I have gathered a posie of other men's flowers and nothing but the thread that binds them is my own."

The dedication in the front of the book says:

"To my son, who shared my love for poetry but thinks his father's taste a little old-fashioned."

* * *

At the beginning of the book in his foreword. In it appears the following:

"This is a purely personal anthology. I have read much poetry; and since I had once a very retentive memory for verse much has remained in my head. I have had less opportunity to read poetry during these late years of war. When I do so, I find that I read the old favorites rather than fresh poets or poems; so that with failing memory it is unlikely that I shall acquire much more by heart. It amuses me lately to set down in a notebook—mainly with a view to discussion with my son, who shares my liking for poetry—the poems I could repeat entire of in great part. I have now collected and arranged the poems I set down. I did it with no idea of publication, but my son and others have suggested that the collection might appeal to a wider circle."

* * *

There are many poems in this volume that might be appropriately quoted in connection with the untimely and heroic death of young Wavell, who, as a true soldier of the Queen, gave his life combatting the terrorism and almost religious fanaticism of the dread Mau Mau revolt.

Near the end of the book the author quotes a poem by Rupert Brooke called "The Dead," and in an explanatory note says:

"I can well remember Lord Allenby repeating this poem to me shortly after he had heard the news that his only son, a boy of great promise, had been killed in action."

The poem is as follows:

"These hearts were woven of human joys and cares,
        Washed marvelously with sorrow, swift to mirth.
The years had given them kindness. Dawn was theirs,
        And sunset, and the colours of the earth.
These had seen movement, and heard music; known
        Slumber and waking; loved; gone proudly friended;
Felt the quick stir of wonder; sat alone;
        Touched furs and flowers and cheeks. All this is ended.

There are waters blown by changing winds to laughter
And lit by the rich skies, all day. And after,
        Frost, with a gesture, stays the waves that dance
And wandering loveliness. He leaves a white
        Unbroken glory, a gathered radiance,
A width, a shining peace, under the night."

* * *

But even more appropriate is another poem, too long to quote here, by Sir Francis Hastings Doyle. It is titled "The Red Thread of Honour," and it must suffice to give Viscount Wavell's explanation for the historical background for the poem. It related to the 13th Volunteers, and English army unit now known as the Somerset Light Infantry, and an encounter they had in fighting in the hill country of India, in what is now Pakistan:

"Those commanders had, as before related, entered a short way into the defile, but from some error, a sergeant and 16 privates of the 13th Volunteers got on the wrong side of what appeared a small chasm and went against a height crowned by the enemy, where the chasm suddenly deepened so as to be impassable. The company from which the sergeant had separated was on the other side, and his officer seeing how strong the hillmen were on the rock, made signs to retire, which the sergeant mistook for gestures to attack, and with inexpressible intrepidity scaled the precipitous height. The robbers waited concealed behind a breast-work on a landing place until 11 of the party came up, and then, being 70 in number, closed in on them. All the 11 had medals, some had three, and in that dire moment proved that their courage at Jellalabad had not been exaggerated by fame. Six of them fell stark, and the others being wounded, were shoved back over the edge and rolled down the almost perpendicular side of the hill; but this did not happen until 17 of the robbers and their commander were laid dead above.

"There is a custom with hillmen, that when a great champion dies in battle, his comrades, after stripping his body, tie a red or green thread around his right or left wrist, according to the greatness of his exploit—the red being most honourable. Here those brave warriors stripped the British dead, and cast the bodies over; but with this testimony of their own chivalric sense of honor and the greatness of the fallen soldiers' courage—each body had a red thread on both wrists."

Surely it must have been a moving occasion this past Christmas Eve when, as the senior Wavell sat among the heroes of all time in the great flagstone hall of Valhalla gazing into the huge fire that roared yellow and scarlet and blue in the chimney throat, he heard a stirring at the other end of the hall and turned to see his own son enter and stride toward him with outstretched arms.

And—(since in Valhalla those things which should be done are counted as done already!)—surely the father's heart must have filled to overflowing when, lowering his eyes, he glimpsed, for the first time, the tiny thread of scarlet that circled each wrist of his beloved and only son!

The Voice and a Christmas Fantasy

I heard a voice from Heaven.
It was the voice of a dog and it said,
"Repent! Repent! for the Kingdom of Heaven is at hand!"

Where are the lean hunters?
Or did they vanish when
Two chickens appeared in each pot
And two cars in each garage?

Where are the ragged revolutionaries?
Or did Brooks Brothers and The Family Clothing Company (nothing
down, two years to pay) destroy them?

Where are the women who birthed a nation
And suckled it while they held a
Rifle in one hand and a skillet in the other?
Have they gone out as the New Look
Came in and the angled hardness of a poised cigarette?

The hills and the valleys
Still bring forth young corn
The trees of the forest
Still clap their hands.

But now in this time
Of russet leaves and under
This troubled cloud of mortality
We cry aloud these questions
In vain, in vain . . .

For the only voice from Heaven
Is the voice of a dog.
And it says

"Repent! Repent!
For the Kingdom of Heaven
Is at hand."

It's Berlin on Christmas morning, the year of our Lord 1943.

A heavy snow has fallen during the night and the city is blanketed in cold whiteness. The city crouches silent in the cold pale blue stillness of dawn. The rubble and wreckage of recent bombings is apparent, although softened and subdued by the gracious coverlet of the clean snow.

Indoors, people are up. They huddle about their meager fires. Some of them, when there are no children about, speak of this festive day, this holiday season. They are aware that in some lands, at least, this day is still one of carols, of the singing of their own "Silent Night," of gaiety and laughter—of heaped up plates of delicious food, steaming and redolent and good, and of flowing bowls—of the bright eyes of children and the glad glowing hearts of those who love children. Then they fall silent again and gaze out the window.

Of a sudden, the air is split by the hoarse scream of sirens. The sound begins low and throaty—basso profundo, and then climbs steeply into a high falsetto, only to swoop down again. The air quivers with the intensity of the warning. At almost the same time, the chattering of the ack-ack guns begins.

Some of the people make for the shelters. Others—either more fatalistic or perhaps merely careless—remain.

And then, sudden and insidious, there comes another sound—the low, ominous growl of many planes. It is a far, dim sound, yet ever nearer. Closer it comes, and closer, until the earth and air are shaken, Then the poor fools gazing out of their windows into that bright Christmas morning there is borne a sight, like of which no man has ever seen.

The sky is filled with bombers. Lancasters and Fortresses lead the way, their quadruple propellers biting hugely, hungrily through the cold, clean spaces fifteen thousand feet up, the sun glinting off the planes as they fly steadily, implacably on. To the north, to the south, they fill the sky. Thousands of planes—every kind of bomber in the Allied arsenal-fly proud and dangerously beautiful in the sunlight, their vapor trails spinning out whitely behind. Occasionally an ack-ack shell strikes home and a plane dips out of formation and falls into a smoking, plummeting dive, or explodes in mid-air.

On and on they come, until at last they cover the city as completely as does the snow. The noise, the imminent death and the horror, is indescribable.

At that moment, on some given signal, their bomb bays swing open, and down, down through the golden light of early morning, plummet packages—not of death and destruction but of food—of bread and tea, of canned milk and every good thing, even striped sticks of candy for the cowering, terror-stricken children of Berlin.

And as that giant host of planes swings to the west and its thunder dims and dies across the winter-locked land, there may be heard dim echoes of sleigh bells, the hollow tollings of cathedral carillons—the overtones of angels singing.

Insane you say! Yes. Yes, we must never, never, you know, take the words of that Carpenter too seriously, and yet . . . it is rather an interesting idea, don't you think?

Memories of 'The TAG'

*"It was late October, there was a smell of smoke upon the air, an
odor of burning leaves, the barking of a dog, a misty red, a pollenated
gold in the rich, fading sorrowful, and exultant light of the day—and far
off, a sound of great wheels pounding on a rail, the wailing whistle and
the tolling bell of a departing train. . ."*

—Thomas Wolfe

It was a day of blue-hazed October, the woods aflame with color, the
crisp air tart with the scent of drying grass and fallen leaves . . . and the
paper told of the death at 101, of Samuel Igou, retired locomotive
engineer of the Tennessee, Alabama and Georgia Railroad.

The memories flowed like wine . . .

The TAG railroad, built near the turn of the century by the late C.E.
James, snakes its way down the Chattanooga Valley, across McLemore's
Cove, through a tunnel in Pigeon Mountain, and thence southward be-
low the eastern flank of Lookout Mountain to Gadsden. The names of
the stations are like the sound of music: Flintstone, Kensington, Blue
Pond, Menlo, Cassandra.

In the mid-twenties the little short-line road was bought for a pittance
by a group of four Chattanoogans: Clayton Smallwood, George Christian, John Paalzow and John Chambliss.

A couple of years later they sold it to a New York syndicate headed
by the prestigious engineering firm of Coverdale and Colpitts.

John Chambliss chose to join the syndicate and retain an interest in
the railroad. Later, Garrison and Mose Siskin acquired stock in the
company, and until his death Garrison was chairman of the board.

About a decade ago, the TAG was acquired by the Southern Railway, and it continues as a wholly-owned Southern subsidiary.

I remember so many things about the TAG:

The scooter was a "Toonerville Trolley" type of gasoline-powered
car that ran from Chattanooga to Gadsden and back each day. Its motor-
man, George Love, a friendly ruddy-faced, squint-eyed character, lived
in Alton Park. The scooter was the only passenger-and-mail-carrying
service the railroad provided.

179

Mr. Shannon, the roadmaster, was huge, Irish and jolly.

"Spud" Fricks and his brother Jeff doubled as both fireman and engineer, the number one engineer being Mr. Igou.

Then there was a huge, fat, happy black man who worked at the Round House in Alton Park.

Back in the early days, the president was H.F. Bohr, who was succeeded by D.E. Hedges (of Hedges Orchard fame). At the time the Southern took over, Macon Tolleson was president.

One of my father's proudest moments was when a new diesel locomotive was named for him, at the insistence of his friend Garrison Siskin.

Trains were always important in our family's life. They took one away to school, or on business, or on pleasure trips . . . and then they brought one home again, which was the best of all.

The distant wind-blown whistle of a steam locomotive pierced the heart: it told of departure and loss, and of the coming again. The clickety-clack of the wheels on the rails lulled one to sleep in the white-linened, green-curtained Pullman berth. And sometimes there was the halt of the train in the middle of the night, when, peering around the drawn shade, you saw the dim-lit station of some unknown town. Then, with a hiss of released airbrakes, the train would jerk slightly and begin to move again.

The names of the famous trains were magic: The Empire Builder, the Wabash Cannonball, the Pan-American, the Super-Chief, and closer home, the Dixie Flyer, the Queen and Crescent, the Royal Palm and the Pelican. A Nashville radio station used to broadcast each night the sound of the screaming whistle and rushing roar of the Pan-American as it passed hear Nashville.

When we children were very small, our father would take us down to Wauhatchie to stand beside the track and wait to see the Dixie Flyer thunder past, showering cinders and stifling us in harsh train smoke, its engineer, Oley Hulse, goggled and gloved, waving in kingly salute.

Not only I, but my brothers, and later my son and a daughter, worked for the TAG, at one time or another. I remember so well riding one night on the locomotive from Gadsden to Chattanooga, and learning how rough a ride it was, and how desperately hard the fireman had to work as he tossed untold shovel-loads of coal into the lurid, gaping mouth of the firebox.

Born of this love of trains—part inherited and part acquired—I wrote, when I was about 18, the first poem I'd ever written that really pleased me. It was about a locomotive and it ended as follows:

" . . . Even the moon knows you, Huge smoky churl.

Long as he hangs there, like
A Christmas tree decoration

Long after lovers and thieves
Are home abed—he sees, in the
Darkness, your yellow eye
And hears the eerie echoes
Of your moans, the subdued
Clicking of your clatter, as
You wallow down the silver rails,
And the pilot star turns to
The moon and drawls: "What's the hurry?"
The sun, the moon-they do not see
The set face of the grim man-thing
Clinging on the seat of the bucking cab—
Squinting along the sweaty sides of the
Boiler, hand on throttle, to see
Whether the light be red or green . . ."

So in this season of the down-turning of the year, I dream of the
faraway and the long ago and am sure that Sam Igou, and Casey Jones,
and Oley Hulse, and all the other brave engineers who have finished
their Last Run, are safely home with their iron horses in that Round-
house in the Sky!

181

The Dream Peddler

Of a sudden, in some miraculous way, the heat is departed and the new coolness, the air redolent with the fragrance of drying grass, speak of autumn. Now there is rain at last, whispering softly down, to freshen the earth and the hearts of men.

Summer is gone, and we know again that time passes. Time passes and the season turns.

It is a nostalgic time—and thinking of memories and the wheel of time, we are reminded of Ed Barnes, recently released from the hospital, and some of his different lives. We have room for only three of them but they are worthy of note.

For years and years Ed Barnes worked behind the ticket counter of the Southern Railway at the Terminal Station.

Those were the days of steam, when the huge chuffing locomotives would ease into the station, hissing steamily; people thronged the platforms and the interior of the station itself and the redcaps sifted through the crowd carrying baggage for the more affluent; the chant of the train caller was heard: "All aboard! Track No. 5 . . . Train No. 41 . . .the Pelican . . .Attalla . . . Birmingham . . . Hattiesburg . . . New Orleans . . . all aboard!"

Ed used to sit behind the caged window and make out tickets, the regular train tickets and also Pullman tickets. The latter were the magic passes to enter the elegance of such exotically named sleeping cars as Mt. Shasta, Bull Run, and Rappahannock.

These were the places of the gold-braided conductors, the white-jacketed pullman porters, and the green hangings that concealed the white linen of the berths where you slept. Lifting the shade of the window of your berth when the train stopped during the night hours in some unknown and mysterious place, you would look out and see an electric light bulb blazing in the lonely darkness beside a shed or a dingy old building, and you would wonder where you were . . . and why . . . and when you would be moving on.

Then, with a sudden hiss of released air brakes and a jerk, the car would begin to move again, slow, easy, and then faster, and soon you would drift back to sleep to the clickity-clack of the wheels on the rail joints.

It was Ed Barnes whose hands delivered to us ordinary people the tickets to great cities, rosy in the early morning sunlight, whose buildings soared steeply up beside the gray-green sea; to prairies, rippling with golden wheat and stretching endlessly over the midlands of America; to the great green mountains and jewelled blue lakes of the Canadian Northwest.

What a life!

But that was only a part.

In the late 40's, after World War II, Ed Barnes retired.

But Ed Barnes wasn't thinking of quitting.

So he opened up his own travel agency in the Read House and continued to help people plan and make trips.

Now he arranged for all kinds of tickets—railroad tickets, airline tickets, steamship tickets. He advised as to itinerary—as to where to go, and how, and when.

His life expanded. His was no longer a matter of earthbound trains. He had at his fingertips the great silver birds whose wings carry one up beyond the clouds and into the bright blue heavens. He also had at his command ocean liners, those floating islands that snuggle briefly alongside the piers of the ports of the world—those liners, tended by small snorting tugs, which, when the time for their departure comes, loose the mournful cry of their whistle and move slowly and majestically out into the stream to meet the swell and dip of the world's oceans.

Romance was his trade: the sunlight falling on the worn walls of ancient towns and cities; the green-loveliness of Alpine valleys, starred with flowers; the winding lanes, and the honeysuckled hedgerows and the sunlight-dappled forests that the heart recognizes even though the eye has never met them before.

As time went on, his brother Victor and his sister-in-law, Miss Hilda, joined him. The three of them were a joy never to be forgotten—figuring schedules, securing reservations, furnishing tickets—and always with a friendliness and a gladness as refreshing as it was true.

Then, a bit over a year ago, Ed Barnes retired again.

But there is still another life that Ed Barnes has lived, all along. He will never retire from it.

He was and is one of the inspirational leaders of the Gideons, that little band of unselfish and devoted Christian men who take on the pragmatic task of helping the work-a-day world discover the glow and serenity and enthusiasm that comes from living (or even trying to live!) a Christian life.

Having spent so much of his different lives arranging for people's journeys, perhaps it is not surprising that Ed Barnes is concerned with plans for the Longest Journey of All!

"Travel," says Freya Stark, "is a search for good days—good days to be gathered like sunshine in grapes, to be trodden and bottled into wine and kept for age to sip at ease beside his fire. If the traveler has vintaged well", she says, "he need trouble to wander no longer; the ruby moments glow in his glass at will."

Somehow, Ed Barnes has always seemed to know this.

And now, whenever we hear the distant thunder of a jet high overhead, or the deep-throated whistle of a ship, or the faraway crying of a train at midnight—we always think of this dream peddler whose various lives have been devoted to making the magic of travel come true for so many.

Thank you, Ed Barnes!

'Arms and A Man'

The bugle call *Taps* is the most haunting and poignant of all. It bears the message "go to sleep" and as someone has said,

"Sleep is an island.
"You retire to it to
"renew your strength
"and come to know
"your soul.
"Death is a larger
"island, but of the
"same qualities . . ."

A few days ago *Taps* sounded for one of the best-loved members of our community.

Known as Father Joe in recent years, Morgan C. Nichols was born in Camden, Miss.

While still a child he was nicknamed Jo-jo for a monkey cartoon character in the weather column of a Memphis paper, and the name stuck.

After attending the University of Alabama and then Howard College, he went to work for Alabama Power Co. and married his college sweetheart, Lib Loyd. They began their married life in a tiny Alabama community which he referred to as Bug Tussle.

Soon thereafter, though, he came to work for Provident Life and Accident Insurance Co. Overcoming extreme timidity, he did so well that he became a senior vice president and a member of the Provident's board of directors.

Joe had an irrepressible sense of impish humor.

On one occasion, while driving hurriedly through Mississippi on the way to his next appointment, he suddenly found himself trapped in a funeral cortege. Frustrated, he stewed over what to do, until, glimpsing a side road ahead which he knew would take him where he wanted to go, he turned onto it and accelerated. After about five minutes, he looked in his rearview mirror and saw—to his horror—the last half of the funeral procession still behind him!

In the mid-50s, shortly after vacationing in Mexico, he decided to leave the business world and enter the Episcopal priesthood.

Completing the required courses at St. Luke's School of Theology at Sewanee, he moved to Memphis, where he worked under the then-bishop of Tennessee.

Several years later he returned to Chattanooga to serve as associate rector at the Church of the Good Shepherd, his home church, and later as rector at Thankful Memorial and priest-in-charge at St. Mary the Virgin in Alton Park. He was a key figure in the establishment of CADAS, providing help to alcoholics and drug abusers.

In all his activities, whether in the business world or the church, his love of people shone through, with his courtliness, his kindness and his understanding.

Several years ago his beloved Lib was stricken with cancer. Following her death he moved into an apartment at St. Barnabas and later into the nursing home there.

During the past few years his memory began to fail, as it does with most of us. But he always recognized me and I continued to delight in going to see him and asking if he could remember the opening line of Virgil's Aeneid, which he had memorized at Sawney Webb's School at Bell Buckle, Tenn.

Joe's face would light up, he would smile that lovely smile and then begin:

"Arma virumque cano, Troiae qui primus ab oris . . ."

"Arms and a man I sing . . ."

How fitting that Joe should remember that—Joe, whose own arms were always outstretched to protect and comfort the bruised souls he saw around him!

In addition to his and Lib's legacy of two beautiful daughters and a bevy of grandchildren, this man will always be remembered by everyone who knew him for his love for all people.

"Arms and a man . . ."

What an epitaph!

Requiescat in pace!

Mr. Sam

Springtime is a magic season. The misty young green of trees, the white of dogwood blossoms, the wine-colored redbud, the lavender of wisteria, the kaleidoscopic songs of birds, all remind us of the poet's

"April, April, laugh they golden laughter

then, the moment after, weep thy golden tears . . ."

Yet, even in such a season there are reminders of mortality.

* * *

Samuel Rees Parry stopped breathing on March 31, 1992 after a long but blessedly painless, wasting away. He would have been 88 this July.

In the hearts of those who knew and loved him, though—and they are legion - Mr. Sam - an American Welshman - will always be alive.

* * *

Wales, the home of Welshmen, is a land of vivid contrast. Between the slate-hard Snowdonia mountains of the north and the coal fields of the south lie rolling green hills, forever dappled by the shadows of white clouds that come sailing in off the Atlantic, like Spanish galleons afloat in a sky-sea of incredible blue.

Wales and its people can be described in two words: strength . . . and tenderness.

Mr. Sam embodied both.

His Welsh ancestors—on both sides—came to America, settling first in Ohio, and then coming South to the Sale Creek-Soddy area, where they opened a coal mine.

About the time of World War I the Parry family moved to the Cameron Hill neighborhood of Chattanooga, and young Sam went to work for the Walsh and Weidner Boiler Company after graduating from City High School.

Soon after, he entered Georgia Tech as the first co-op student to go there from Chattanooga. He worked four weeks, went to school four weeks, repeating the cycle until he won his engineering degree, and came home to the Boiler Company, which by then was a part of Combustion Engineering Company.

When I first met him it was in the early '30's. He was in the office of my grandfather, J.B. Sizer, who was the lawyer for Combustion and also senior partner in our family firm. After WW2, Mr. Sam succeeded A.J. Moses, his boss and friend, as general manager of the Combustion plant here, and in 1959 was promoted to Executive Vice President in charge of all Combustion plants in the united States with his office in New York. After only a few months, though, he decided he wanted to stay in Chattanooga—so he took early retirement to join his (and my) close friend Dan Overmyer, as Executive Vice President of Chattanooga Box and Lumber Company. Some years later, when that company was acquired by Temple Industries of Texas, he went with Chattanooga Glass, and Dorsey, as consultant, and also became consultant to his good friend Alex Guerry of Chattem Drugs. In addition, for years he served as a member of the Electric Power Board, and was its chairman for a term . . . and then, when he resigned, agreed to stay on as an advisor to the Board, and continued in that capacity until his death.

Mr. Sam shared the feeling of Tennyson's "Ulysses" in

"How dull it is to pause, to make an end,
    to rust unburnished, not to shine in use!"

But it is not for his business or professional career that he was so unforgettable . . . it was as a "people person" and philosopher.

Foremost in his people-relationships was his family: his wife, Eva, their son Sam—a quiet-spoken member of the faculty of the Naval Post-Graduate School in Monterey, California, (and a key figure in the strategic military councils of the United States), and his son's family. Also in his close family group were his two sisters, both of whom survive him.

How did Mr. Sam have so much left to give to the rest of us?

He was loved by more people than could ever be counted . . . people of all sorts: the high and the mighty, the weak and the lowly, the black and the white. And he was the same to all.

While at Combustion he was admired, respected and trusted by everyone. During a Labor Board hearing at the Federal building, the business agent of the union, pointing to Mr. Sam, said for all to hear, "I'd rather have _his_ word than a contract!"

Again, typical was the time he came to the plant one morning and was told by the shop foreman that the night before an employee had ruined a piece of equipment that would cost the company thousands of dollars . . . adding that the employee had been notified he was to be fired.

Mr. Sam listened . . . then said "Send him in to see me."

When the man came, Mr. Sam spoke in his always easy, relaxed way:

"Well, son . . .tell me about it."

The man said:

"Mr. Sam, my wife's been real sick of late, and yesterday our little boy took sick too, and 'most died . . .I reckon I had all that on my mind . . . Anyhow—it was my fault . . . my mistake."

Mr. Sam looked at him, slowly shook his head, smiled, and said:

"You're not fired, son . . . get on back to your job."

All sorts of people have been helped in all sorts of ways by what Mr. Sam did for them.

More than thirty years ago he gave a talk to the Tennessee Industrial Personnel Conference. He titled the talk "A Bridge To Build." It was about what it took to build this America of ours . . . and at the end he read this poem:

> An old man, traveling a lone highway
> Came at the evening, cold and grey,
> To a chasm deep and wide.
> The old man crossed in the twilight dim
> For the sullen stream held no fears for him,
> But he turned when he reached the other side
> And builded a bridge to span the tide.
>
> 'Old man,' cried a fellow pilgrim near,
> 'You are wasting your strength with building here.
> Your journey will end with the ending day
> And you never again will pass this way.
> You have crossed the chasm, deep and wide—
> Why build you a bridge at eventide?'
>
> Then the builder raised his old grey head—
> 'Good friend, on the path I have come,' he said
> 'There followeth after me today
> A youth whose feet will pass this way.
> This stream which has been as naught to me
> To that fair-haired boy may a pitfall be . . .
> He too must cross in a twilight dim—
> Good friend, I am building this bridge for him.'

* * *

Mr. Sam was, above all else, a Bridge Builder.

Clear and clean as the mountain brooks that tumble down the rocky falls in North Wales, Mr. Sam always held to his belief in the basic God-laws and natural laws that have governed since the world began.

Rare wisdom was his . . . and he deserved, more than anyone else I've even known, a PhD. in Common Sense.

Once, years ago, I heard him say that "luck is when preparation meets opportunity."

But it was God's grace that gave all of us Mr. Sam!